"When I put this book down, I felt like I'd just come from coffee with Tracey and Adele—the best kind of coffee with friends, where you stay for hours and tell the truth, where you're given a gentle but challenging vision for the path ahead, where vulnerability and wisdom clear a space for better ways of living."

Shauna Niequist, author of *Bread & Wine*

"'Your life matters and isn't just about you.' This sentence is a good summary of what Calhoun and Bianchi have to say in *True You*. These are words of dual truth that all women need to hear and believe—and they're rarely spoken in our world. With empathy and sisterly candor, these two women call us to what we already want to be and give us the courage to pursue our true selves."

Amy Simpson, author, *Anxious: Choosing Faith in a World of Worry*, editor, Christianity Today's GiftedforLeadership.com

"True You does better than provide the 'right' answers: it asks the right questions. This book is a must-read for the thinking woman, one who wants to live out fully who God created her to be."

Caryn Rivadeneira, author of *Broke: What Financial Desperation Revealed About God's Abundance*

"Every woman has a story, but not all of us know how to take what we have experienced and learned and known and tell that story. This wonderful book helps a woman find her voice—one that is neither too loud nor too soft; one that is truly God-given and unique. Through stories, experiences and very practical applications, Tracey Bianchi and Adele Ahlberg Calhoun help women 'lean in' to all that God has for them. A great book to share with a friend or a study group and one that every woman will find uplifting and helpful."

Dale Hanson Bourke, author of the *Skeptic's Guide Series* and *Embracing Your Second Calling*

"A refreshingly honest and encouraging book! You will laugh and cry. You will be comforted and challenged. You will be sobered by all the ways women are held back and hold themselves back, and yet hopeful that women can yet become all God created us to be. While I long for the day in which such books will no longer be needed, I am grateful Adele and Tracey have teamed up to write this one."

Ruth Haley Barton, Transforming Center, author of *Longing For More*

"I experienced *True You* as a call to authenticity, weaving together the vulnerability of story-telling, bold vision, plus, a quality often missing among visionaries, common sense. The authors' wisdom reached to the soul center, from which our work in the world can best be unleashed."

Helen LaKelly Hunt, activist and co-founder of Women Moving Millions

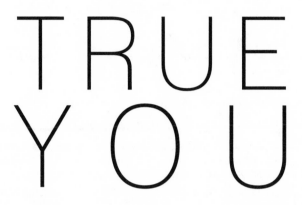

TRUE YOU

Overcoming Self-Doubt and Using Your Voice

ADELE AHLBERG CALHOUN
& TRACEY D. BIANCHI

IVP Books

An imprint of InterVarsity Press
Downers Grove, Illinois

InterVarsity Press
P.O. Box 1400, Downers Grove, IL 60515-1426
ivpress.com
email@ivpress.com

InterVarsity Press® is the book-publishing division of InterVarsity Christian Fellowship/USA®, a movement of students and faculty active on campus at hundreds of universities, colleges and schools of nursing in the United States of America, and a member movement of the International Fellowship of Evangelical Students. For information about local and regional activities, visit intervarsity.org.

All Scripture quotations, unless otherwise indicated, are taken from THE HOLY BIBLE, NEW INTERNATIONAL VERSION®, NIV® Copyright © 1973, 1978, 1984, 2011 by Biblica, Inc.™ Used by permission. All rights reserved worldwide.

While any stories in this book are true, some names and identifying information may have been changed to protect the privacy of individuals.

Cover design: Cindy Kiple
Interior design: Beth McGill
Images: colored socks: Louise Geoghegan/Getty Images
         glass slipper: © Mega_Pixel/iStockphoto

ISBN 978-0-8308-4315-2 (print)
ISBN 978-0-8308-9764-3 (digital)

Printed in the United States of America

Library of Congress Cataloging-in-Publication Data
Calhoun, Adele Ahlberg, 1949-
  True you : overcoming self-doubt and using your voice / Adele
Ahlberg Calhoun and Tracey D. Bianchi.
      pages cm
  Includes bibliographical references.
  ISBN 978-0-8308-4315-2 (pbk. : alk. paper)
  1. Christian women—Religious life. 2. Self-doubt. 3.
Self-perception in women—Religious aspects. 4.
Self-perception—Religious aspect—Christianity. I. Title.
  BV4527.C25 2014
  248.8'43--dc23
                                                    2014033484

P   20   19   18   17   16   15   14   13   12   11   10   9   8   7   6   5   4   3   2   1
Y   31   30   29   28   27   26   25   24   23   22   21   20   19   18   17   16   15

For Annaliese and Lilly

"I don't want to get to the end of my life and

find that I lived just the length of it.

I want to have lived the width of it as well."

DIANE ACKERMAN

CONTENTS

INTRODUCTION

❧

Suzanne Heintz travels the world with mannequins—actual, life-sized, gush-over-in-a-store-window mannequins. An artist who grew up in New York, Heintz has been traveling the world for fourteen years with her plastic husband, Chauncey, and plastic daughter, Mary Margaret. Her work is whimsical and provocative, her photos a riot. You can catch them skiing, road tripping or huddled around a bistro table in Paris. Heintz is a single woman who launched her global escapades from a place of frustration. After decades of feeling the pressure to get married, settle down and raise a family, she decided to call out our culture's obsession with tying a woman's value to her roles in marriage and family. Heintz and her plastic trio expose the tremendous pressure women face to live, act, love, learn and achieve in culturally acceptable ways.[1]

Pressure to perform and conform starts young. Elementary-age girls are grossly aware of where they don't measure up and how they are lacking. Before they even hit puberty, the life of tenacious striving begins. The expectations are overwhelming, and many younger girls face feelings of isolation, anxiety and loneliness, triggered by the pressure of it all. According to the National Alliance on Mental Illness, women struggle with depression at twice the rate of men.[2]

In attempts to keep up appearances we all but drink rocket fuel for breakfast, and in the haste and compulsion our ability to keep in touch with the truest parts of ourselves is erased. If we get a quiet moment we are ambushed with doubts. *Who am I? What if I don't want (or am not able) to raise a family? Am I smart/strong/valuable enough to do something different with my life? What if I don't want to marry? What if my marriage ends in a fiery divorce? What about my education and career? What if I'm a lousy parent? What if friendships slip?*

In a culture that urges women to strive toward impossible ideals, many of us feel overwhelmed and insecure. The message to achieve more and look fantastic doing it pushes us into compulsive busyness, so much so that the close connections and meaningful conversations we long for never happen. The poet John Donne once penned, "No man is an island,"[3] but the reality is that many women feel like they are on one. Heintz says, "For women, the path to fulfillment is not through one thing, it's through all things: education, career, home, family, accomplishment, enlightenment. If any one of those things is left out, it's often perceived that there's something wrong with your life. We are somehow never enough, just as we are."[4]

What would it be like if we found ourselves in a conversation about the fact that each one of us is actually enough? Just as we are in this very moment. Today. Now. That inside of us God whipped up the perfect cocktail of artist, poet, athlete, friend, lover, learner, so that we do not actually have to strive. What if we took some time to catch our collective breath, calm our souls and discover the *true you*? Might we live fuller, less isolated, less pressure-cracked lives?

This small book is our attempt to claim some new ground into real self-clarity. We call it finding and embracing the true you. The path to this deepest, truest part of ourselves becomes clearer when we consider who we are and what holds us back. When someone doesn't mirror back the image we hold of ourselves, what do we do? What happens when we settle into a deck chair at night and find a moment to catch a glimpse of our often-anemic souls? How do things like friendship, competition, prayer, rest, justice, aging, and image nourish or starve along the way to a true you? This book is a journey into some of the places where women struggle. It is an attempt to gain awareness and solidarity on the deep realities women face regardless of age, life stage or generational affiliations. It is a reminder, a note to self and the world, that there is an objective, substantial, beloved *true you* waiting to be known in each of us.

OUR STORY

For more than a dozen years we served on staff at the same church. We would often flop on the dusty, retro floral couch in Adele's office and chat about everything from ministry to justice, sex, politics, theology and our favorite wine. We talked about women, and culture, and families, and being stressed, and biblical authority, and writing a book together. This gave us a tremendous sense of solidarity and the confidence that someone had our back.

Now we live in different parts of the country, but our friendship is a gift we keep giving each other. Though we are separated by twenty-five years and are at different stages of life, we have helped one another live into what is real and true and good about us. We also recognize that we live in places and at a time in history that afford us the luxury to talk about these issues. Millions of women do not have this same opportunity. We are white girls from massive urban areas in the United States, Boston and Chicago. We've suffered our share of angst, pain and setbacks, but we recognize that the following conversations sometimes reflect the "luxuries" of our lives (opportunities for education, the right to vote, access to resources, etc.).

This book focuses on the lives of many women in our unique twenty-first-century context. There are so many women and stories we don't know and cannot pretend that we've heard. So it's not about all women. And it is not a treatise against men. The irony of this conversation is that talking about women and culture inevitably means discussing men, because men vigorously inform our culture. It gets chancy at times. We are or have daughters, sisters, friends, colleagues, mothers, cousins, grandmothers and aunts. We know their stories. We commiserate with their struggles and how they, too, in their own ways, wrestle with what lies within these pages. Our hope for this book is that you, too, will know someone has your back.

HOW THIS BOOK WORKS

There are several ways you might use this book:

- Read it with a friend and chat about the practices at the end of each chapter

- Read it with a small group

- Use it as a Bible study and focus on the set of Bible study questions in the appendix

- Read it with a guy—a colleague, brother, husband, father or friend—and invite him into a deeper understanding of women's struggles today

- Ask your pastor to read it

Each chapter begins with a six-word story. Hemingway is rumored to have said that his best story was only six words long: "For sale. Baby shoes. Never worn." We have asked a variety of women to offer six-word stories for each topic, drawn from the experiences of their lives. We have kicked in our own six-word stories too.

The end of each chapter includes a set of practices and journal questions. The practices include things you can do each week. If you prefer more tactile ways to engage with the conversation, these are for you. For verbal processors there are a variety of journal questions included. Finally, we are two women among millions who are smarter and wiser than us, so we've included an appendix of other voices: additional books, videos, websites and resources to further your exploration and understanding. We don't necessarily endorse all of these voices, but they are representative of our culture. We need to be aware of how they shape the women and world around us.

There is no way to write a book about women that does not alienate or at least irritate someone. But our bottom line is this: We believe in the authority of Scripture. We love God. We love women. And we want women to be free to bring their *true you* to the world.

PART ONE

True Relationships

YOUR ONE TRUE STORY

Be you. No one else can.

NANCY CREMER

Pop culture, arguably, is the most powerful influencer of our views and lifestyles. And yet, like the water fish swim in, gravity or the very air we breathe, it is a given that goes unnoticed. We don't think much about breathing, it just happens, albeit some twenty-one thousand times per day. We may believe our views on gender, politics, family, God or even our favorite sweatshirt are our own, but they are more likely a rich combination of influences both noted and unnoted. We've inhaled a combination of influences that become what we say, believe and hold as truth. Uncovering the true you means recognizing any broken, false ideals that we breathe in.

THE BECHDEL TEST

Elements of culture can either empower or erase the voices and value of women. Each year we suck in our culture's views on women through the box-office hits that rake in hundreds of millions. Movies, music, videos and celebrities inform everything from our slang, banter and fashion to our obsession with certain automobiles, spring break destinations and shoes. All these easily inform and shape how women view themselves and interact with one another.

The Bechdel Test is a tool that illustrates this point. This diagnostic evaluates movies on three simple criteria:

1. The movie must have at least two [named] women in it.

2. Those women must talk to one another.

3. About something other than a man.

No big deal, right? According to the Internet Movie Database (IMDb) there will have been around 268,000 movies produced from 1888 to 2017. Only forty-seven hundred of those movies pass the Bechdel test. That's only 1.7 percent of all films![1] This seems absurd given how most women we know actually live out their lives. Honestly, does the topic of men come up 98.3 percent of the time you talk to your girlfriends?

Neither of us noticed that so many of the films we love feature women who hardly speak to one another about anything other than men. [Caveat: interestingly, at times a film that contains positive messages for women does not pass the test, while an occasional film that degrades women does pass.] We do not believe the lives of women are meant to be vacuous or exploited. Yet the narrative that apparently plays to our culture's imagination is that it's not okay to be a woman who is single, confident, ready to speak up, or at all content without a man. If you want to be any of these things (or heck, talk to another woman about something other than a man!), something must be wrong with you. With films hammering away at this message, is it any wonder girls and women struggle with self-identity?

Consider for a moment a few Disney movies:

• *Finding Nemo.* The mother dies in the first few minutes.

• *The Little Mermaid.* Lonely Ariel wants to be part of another world; her friends are fish.

• *Tangled.* Rapunzel is kidnapped from her real mother and locked up alone in a tower without friends.

- *Snow White.* Her best friends are seven little men!

- *Cinderella.* Her wretched stepmother and stepsisters are enemies, and other than the prince and a few mice, she is alone.

This list could go on and on. Why are there so shockingly few examples of close friendships between girls, mothers, women? Thankfully, the 2013 Disney release *Frozen* tells the story of how two sisters strengthen their fidelity to one another (and yet, the mother once again dies early on in the film and there is still a significant focus on romantic interests). While recent releases like this represent an encouraging trend, the overwhelming majority of movies still feature narrow, unrealistic or limited female characters and relationships.

Most women don't need a diagnostic to reveal how tough it is to find and hold on to their true selves. From executives to first-year college students, from bold media mavens to women silenced by violence or abuse, we live in a world where it is assumed the trajectory of a woman's life points toward a man. This applies to women both inside and outside faith communities. To be fair, men *are* part of our stories. Fathers, brothers, dads, husbands, friends. Men and women together make up life as we know it. But, when it is assumed that the center of a woman's universe is a man, and that she must spend her time, money, education and energy trying to capture or keep that man, what are we left with? What if we had true conversations about our lives—a film reel about how capable, strong, brilliant, talented and undeniably amazing women actually are, regardless of their status as daughter, sister, wife or mother? What if instead we heard stories about our status as children of God and divine image bearers? What if we told stories about our true selves?

WHAT IS A STORY?

Tracey's friend Constance is an animated storyteller. When she begins to retell an adventure Constance flings her arms up, lowers her voice

and looks with great intensity into the eyes of her listeners—as if the
maestro just cued up a John Williams soundtrack. Thick and weighty,
the red velvet curtains part, and Constance begins her tale. Her voice
rises and falls in a cadence as she unpacks details, drawing you relentlessly toward the climax and closure. She could make pumping gas
sound riveting—like the Sundance Film Festival.

Constance's stories surge with freedom and tenacity, boldly har-
nessing and giving voice to the oddities and nuances of life that gen-
erally fly by unnoticed. Most of us are not as outspoken as Constance.
When I (Tracey) look at her I wonder if I have any stories to tell. She
makes me nervous to tell my stories.

What does my life say when compared to hers? She is a college
professor, an accomplished mountaineer—she's traveled the world.
She hangs out with people whose stories include expeditions up
Everest, while I kick back and plot my next trip to Target. Many of us,
out of fear and uncertainty, are inclined to leave the storytelling of life
to others. Yet, when we do this, it means some strong, true stories of
women lie dormant while the A-list narrative rolls on.

"Stories" are simply the way we share our learnings and under-
standings about our world. They ache for an audience. They come in
brilliant prose and barely audible grunts: verbal, painted, blogged,
sung, tweeted or whispered around a campfire. They can be belted out
on a platform like a polished First Lady, or they can be hidden, locked
up in journals, picked up by a great-granddaughter five decades later.
Each life is a story to be told. True stories tell others:

- This is what I know is true.

- This is what my heart aches for.

- This is how I survive when I hit a bad curve.

- This is where I got it wrong.

- This is the place I misunderstood and misjudged.

- This is why I get up every morning.
- This is how I found God in my story.

We may not wax eloquent like Constance, but we all have stories rattling around, clanging and banging together, waiting for the right moment to be loosed. You don't have to wait for your life to be all grown up or fixed up before you can tell your stories. And you don't have to know the ending or have a neat little moral to tie it all up. I love John Green's *The Fault in Our Stars* for this exact reason. He leaves us wondering.

We learn at an early age which stories matter to our culture. Happy stories. Funny stories. Feel-good stories with fabulous endings. Favored-sibling stories. Winning stories. When our stories don't fit these categories, we doubt them. Some seem too small, too old/young, too private, too impossible. Yet in God's eyes every story is needed. Leave your story untold and the epic tome of human history has a few deleted chapters. When we refuse to tell our stories (to safe people), we rob our sisters, friends and daughters of lessons that may help them to live out the "truest you" in their own lives.

Women's history blogger Shelby Knox says, "I looked up the lives of the women before me because I needed to know that women before had faced obstacles seemingly as insurmountable (and most often much more so!) and came out triumphant. I looked up the lives of the women before me because I needed their sisterhood, their guidance, their solidarity, their example."[2] Our stories help us navigate everything from birth to death, adolescence to breast cancer. Stories help us answer questions:

- Is this normal?
- Am I normal?
- Am I alone?
- Does my story matter to this world?
- Does my story matter to God?

ONE UNREPEATABLE LIFE

Adele's friend Helen LaKelly Hunt wrote her PhD thesis on seventy-five women whose stories shaped their world. These stories remind us that we each have one unique, unrepeatable life—a life that can be lived with gratitude and intentionality. Take Rosa Louise Parks, the now-famous woman who hopped a bus in Montgomery, Alabama, in December of 1955 and refused the driver's order to give up her seat to a white passenger. Hunt quotes Parks, "People always say that I didn't get up because I was tired, . . . but that isn't true. I was not tired physically. . . . No, the only tired I was, was tired of giving in."[3] Rosa Parks was not automatically courageous. She grew up fearing the KKK who haunted her house in the night. Her grandfather stood between her and that terror with a loaded shotgun.

Yet for Parks there was also a story that stood between her and the KKK—a story someone dared to tell that gave her courage, a Bible story she learned as a child: the story of a God who loved and freed people from a tyrant Pharaoh in Egypt who enslaved them. Parks once told the *New York Times*, "I remember finding such comfort and peace while reading the Bible. . . . I learned people should stand up for rights, just as the children of Israel stood up to the Pharaoh."[4]

Rosa risked standing up to the Pharoahs of racism because she knew she was part of a bigger story. She became a catalyst that shaped Martin Luther King Jr. and provided initial momentum for the US Supreme Court to rule that racial segregation in all forms of public transportation was unconstitutional. Surely Rosa never imagined we'd still be telling her story. She was utterly ordinary in so many ways, which proves we don't need a swarm of lobbyists or a million bucks of influence for some God-sized good to happen through us. God needed one thing: a woman who wasn't afraid to use her voice, to step into her true you and dare a different ending to her story.

Each of us gets a one-of-a-kind, unrepeatable chance to live out our true you. We get the story of our soul—the story of how God created a true you and how that God works for our good and our growth. Through betrayals, successes, interruptions, suffering and rebellions, nothing is wasted. No matter what has happened there is holy wisdom to be found. Your life matters and isn't just about you. Your one mangled, mixed-up, unrepeatable life is for your friends, your roommates, your family, your neighbors, your God and the generations to come. Your life is like a stone skipped across a pond. It swiftly grazes the surface, sinks and disappears, but the ripples go on out long after the stone is gone.

CLAIM AUTHORSHIP

Begin to own your story as a way of knowing the true you, even the dark, depressing chapters that you want to keep anonymous, because they are true about you. True stories of women are often historically absent, forgotten or diminished. Yet all these stories—yours, ours, Rosa's, your mama's—belong to God's cosmic history book.

We both love that the Bible is a book of stories. God is not a cosmic killjoy with a rigid manual on religious theory or dogma. When God came in person, in Jesus, it was as a master storyteller. Jesus told stories that disarmed listeners in ways rote teaching did not. The very life of Jesus is the story we keep telling.

God's story reveals how much we matter. Divine intention surrounds our presence here. We each have freedom to write our own story, and we can tell it from a point of gratitude or bitterness, trust or fear, anger or hope. It's up to you. Are you embracing your story as it unfolds, even if wincing a bit? Do you constantly compare your story to someone else's seemingly better life? Jesus once told Peter that his story would include hard and unchosen things. Peter panicked and focused instead on his friend John. He pointed, "'Lord, what about him?' Jesus answered, 'If I want him to remain alive until I return, what is that to you? You must follow me'" (John 21:20-22). John's story was his own, none of Peter's business. He had his own adventure to live.

And it turned out to be nothing less than a story about moving from arrogance to martyrdom (tradition holds that Peter was eventually crucified upside down). The story Peter tried to avoid shaped the very foundation of church history. God used Peter's *true you*.

EXODUS STORIES

Consider the tales that have shaped you deeply. As amazing as Oprah's, Jessica Jackley's or Sheryl Sandberg's story might be, more likely than not a roommate, teacher, family member, neighbor or colleague who cared enough to write you into their life had the most profound impact on you. Their interest in your story, and willingness to share theirs, gives you strength. Consider the unfolding stories of women you know who are rising above generations of alcoholism or establishing nonprofits to serve others or holding families together as single parents.

An exodus story is a tale that moves us from some wilderness to a place of transformation and sense of our truest selves. Exodus stories give us hope that: we won't always be the same; our lives are infused with meaning; there is beauty and gift in who we are and what we bring; we can write better endings; and we can stay true to who God made us to be.

Your exodus story captures the essence of you (up to now) as well as the presence of God on your path. It is etched with dreams, memories, idiosyncrasies, disappointments, pathologies, passions and relationships. This unique account of you and your journey with God is sheer unrepeatable gift.

God moved Israel from famine and slavery to freedom and plenty, and God reminds Israel to remember and retell the gift of her exodus story. This ancient story shapes the Jewish community to this day. It is the saga of God's power to rescue both then and now. Israel's story was never meant to be just for them. It was to be a story that could inspire others to risk on God. And believe it or not that is what God intends our stories to be too.

We each have an exodus story filled with struggle and wonder, stuckness and growth as we move to the truest places inside of us. God invites us to reach deep for our courage so we can retell the stories of how we found God in the fragments, splintered shards and unrealized dreams. Our stories become part of what God is doing in the world and throughout history.

Fanny Crosby, though blinded by an incompetent doctor at six weeks of age, wrote over eight thousand hymns. These songs tell her exodus story. Her lyrics unpack challenges, loneliness, joys and pain. They evidence how she found God and knew she was not alone. When we bring our souls out of hiding, our stories can do the same. When we don't tell our stories it is easy to feel unknown, uncelebrated, alone. Loneliness lurks where stories go unreceived and unspoken.

Be assured that there are people who need your story—it belongs to the archives of God's own story. It is our shared passion that stories of women be told, celebrated and passed on to the glory of God. This happens when we focus on what is true in each of us, and takes us beyond a culture that would have us believe that only certain stories matter.

JOURNAL AND PRACTICE

1. Honor your exodus story by creating a collage (or a board on Pinterest) that depicts some of the chapters in your journey. Share your collage and tell your story to a friend.

2. Be open and attentive to the people coming in and out of your life. Do you find yourself drawn to another woman who seems approachable? Does she have overlap with your life in "coincidental" ways? If the moment comes, reach for your courage and share a chapter of your life with her.

3. Ask a woman you know who seems to be finding her strength and words to tell you her story, good or bad. When she is finished,

thank her for the gift. Tell her what her story means to you. Share
what you learn about yourself from listening to her story.

4. Write down the bits of your own unrepeatable life. How have
you moved from some stuckness to a new place? What is your
exodus story? Let the following questions bring light and healing
to your journey:

- What do I love to do?

- What did I come to believe about myself as a child?

- What voices of encouragement and love have come my way?
Who has believed in me when I didn't believe in myself?

- What lies have shaped my life? Where have I been in
bondage, afraid and unfree?

- What is uniquely mine to give away?

- What God sightings have been posted along my path?

5. For a lighter approach to journaling, write at the top of a piece of
paper, "Once upon a time there was a girl . . ." Make up an adventure about your life, perhaps reclaiming a dream you once had.
Where might you go if you had all the time and financial resources
you needed? Whom might you visit? Would you relax? Fight for
justice? Travel light? Include a few of your most treasured people?
What would it mean to be more open to a real adventure in your
life right now?

6. If you were to put your life into a six-word story, what would
it say? Write a paragraph for each word.

7. What is at the heart of your story with God at this moment? How
do you feel about God, and what is your understanding of who
God is? Is there a prayer that holds your concern and desire? Write
this prayer.

2

TRUE SISTERS

Ten year neighbor, became friends today.

LIVINGLIFEBACKWARDS,
SIX-WORD MEMOIRS WEBSITE

⤜∾

As a young child I (Tracey) would tear up the neighborhood with a trusted band of gal pals that included my sister and the freckle-faced girls who lived across the street. Our summer days were of the idyllic, all-American variety, complete with pool passes, purple banana-seat bicycles and the audacity to overcharge passersby for lemonade. I took for granted that when I rang the neighbors' doorbell they actually wanted to come out and play with me. As years passed I learned that while some friends were always home, the doors of life seemed to go increasingly unanswered. Sometimes all you are allowed to do is peer in through the windows; not everyone considers you an appealing playmate, and in fact, some go out of the way to ensure your exclusion from the neighborhood games.

At age eight I found that doors of friendship could slam shut. Two of my "friends" decided that we should each tell one another who we liked the best. To my chagrin, they decided they liked each other best. My self-esteem evaporated and cosmic loneliness swallowed me whole. Little girls can have such enormous feelings! Later, when one of the girls went home, the other looked at my crushed face and said, "You are really my best friend." But it was too late. The ache inside was already throbbing, radiating out. The gaping feeling of being excluded from a flock of friends flooded my wound of not being chosen. My friend Julie Baier recently reminded me that sororities, teams, cliques and clubs often require tryouts to determine one's value to the group. She also noted how we have to pass the test, meet the (ongoing) membership requirements and then pay the dues once we are in. It's a lot. Friendship is definitely not a "no-cut" sport. For our true selves to flourish and be celebrated we all need trusted companions to help find our way. It's rarely easy to find these connections, but they are essential to bring out the truest you.

GETTING CUT

Both the wounds and joys of friendship impact the ability of our true you to be known. We can be turned out of a heart we once belonged to the very instant someone better, perhaps seemingly an upgraded version of ourself, comes along. Sometimes women pull away and judge without explaining why. Others invite us into the secret, true, holy places of their hearts, and we win this cosmic mega lottery, the victory and gift of friendship. Whether we feel as though we've won that lottery or still find ourselves clinging to a tattered ticket, most of us have struggled at some point to find our way with female friends. Emily Dickinson's poem describes the little passive-aggressive stings and bigger losses friendship can bring.

> My friend must be a Bird—
> Because it flies!
> Mortal, my friend must be,
> Because it dies!
> Barbs has it, like a Bee!

Ah, curious friend!
Thou puzzlest me![1]

If you have moved a lot, you may be the bird that flies. The terrain of your friendships shifts. Some "best" friends puzzle us with their silence once we are no longer physically in the same town. Less-close sisters surprise us with their loyalty when others have long since stopped calling. We wonder whom we puzzle with barbs. Is it something I said? Who has winced or cried because of me? Finding good friends means thinking more than twice about how to be a good, true friend back.

Sisters without barbs help pull out the truest you—friends who consider our quirks, excessive humanness and vulnerabilities endearing, or at the very least, sufferable. These bosom friends add peace-filled words to our stories and offer their true selves in return. They cheer along the sidelines of our lives; they write us into a narrative of belonging. They embody the kinds of friendship represented in *The Sisterhood of the Traveling Pants* or *Anne of Green Gables*. These friends remind us that God never intended us to go at life alone. Our desire to journey with others has holy origins. Even those who don't believe in God and would not necessarily call this impulse "holy" agree that this desire exists.

We both resonate with Claire Luchette, a writer and editor from Chicago whose article for *Bustle* kept us nodding.

You probably have at least one friend that you tell everyone about. You wear her sweater and feel more whole, you talk about how awesome she is at yoga and making nachos, and soon you're gushing to strangers about that time you ate pizza together in a public bathroom in a foreign city at 1:00 a.m. She has your mom's cell phone number, and they casually text. For many of us, these friendships aren't optional—they're essential for survival. They may be more intimate and valuable than our romantic relationships.[2]

How do we arrive in this sort of friendship space? It sounds so enticing, but is it possible?

THE GOODNESS OF BELONGING

We both confess to feeling frantic when we sense we don't belong. Decades after seventh grade, navigating adult friendships still can feel like middle school. We like to think it is not just our neuroses but something so human that it reaches back to creation—to the very beginning of belonging. God started our human story by creating environments first: light and dark, day and night, sky and water, sea and land. In the following days God filled each environment with what *belonged* to it. The sky belonged to the sun, moon, stars, supernovas and black holes. God said, "It is good." The sea teemed with whales, hermit crabs and neon fish, and God reiterated, "It is good." The land belonged to robins, wildebeests and human beings. "It is good." Everything belongs, and God calls it all "very good."

Still there is one thing God finds "not good." It is being alone, solitary—without a tribe, family or friend to call one's own. This "not good" stood even though Adam had God for a friend! It wasn't that God "wasn't enough." It was that God created us to *belong* to others. Sometimes we are told this belonging can only happen in marriage— that the only way to not be alone and to reflect the image of God is to say "I do." This misunderstanding has pushed millions into empty marriages and aloneness. It's not just married couples who belong. For many—even Jesus—friendship answers the ache to belong. Without friends to belong to we warp and ache and are alone. The journey to true friendships begins with knowing that we were designed for this— that our true you is wired for connectivity.

This universal longing to belong fuels popular culture, which both captures the desire and makes me ache over where I am lacking. I wish I had the sort of sibling friendships like those on *Parenthood. Grey's Anatomy,* featuring the witty banter and close friendship of Meredith

Grey and Christina Yang, captured top ratings because their closeness is attractive to us. These shows leave us hoping that we will end up around a table of BFFs, just like them.

Yet scraping together a few soul-shaping companions can be anything but easy. Adolescence can be harsh and friends fickle. We may wonder if adults will be kinder; but honestly, the loneliness of childhood can haunt us into adulthood and even escalate. Anne Lamott suggests, "Most of the time, all you have is the moment, and the imperfect love of the people around you."[3] But sometimes we don't even have that. Many women, despite effort and longing, feel friendless. My (Adele) own transient life has meant making new friends again and again. For the record I hate, hate how hard it is. Each time I move I wonder who will make space for me in their heart and their circle. How long will it take me to belong in this new environment and become part of a new story? It gives me hope to know that we are all designed for community.

A few years ago one of Tracey's childhood gal pals left, and she ached for the woman who could trace the history of her laugh lines and the boys she had dated. She wanted back the woman who knew the food in her snack cabinets and where the Christmas tree once stood in her childhood home. The collective memory, the sense that Tracey had of knowing this friend and being known by her, was truncated. It's hard to find a place to begin again, or to begin for the first time. We move and shift and have to drag ourselves through this time and time again.

FACEBOOK OR FACE TIME?

In a world where initiative, energy, curiosity and time are all endangered, this beginning again or starting from scratch to build a friendship feels nearly impossible. Face-to-face interactions and time spent in the same physical space are vanishing commodities, so many of us log on to connect. It's up for debate how social media ultimately affects our friendships. There are lots of opinions on this one. Facebook friends are far easier. I (Tracey) have many what I call "drive-by Facebook friends," like the girl I ran cross-country with in high school. It's been years since I've seen her, but I "accept" her friend request, and for that moment it's sophomore year all over again. I giggle as fond memories eventually lead me to look people up in an old yearbook. She lives out east now, on her second career and in a snappy urban loft. I post an encouraging note on her wall and then log off. There it ends. A drive-by moment.

To keep casual friends all we have to do is click "like" or "follow," but do all these posts add up to a conversation? Yes and no. How do I tell if the images my former cross-country friend is putting out there are real or spin? It sure looks nice to be her. I want to be her friend, both on Facebook and living in the loft next door and going out for Ethiopian food together. But who is she really these days?

I (Adele) have precisely 595 friends on Facebook. On my birthday I happily scroll through their birthday wishes, but sitting at my friend Cynthia's table for a birthday dinner is something I can't scroll through. I see her face and am in her presence. When she smiles I see the happiness. When her eyes go serious I know she is thinking about what I've said. And when she tears up I understand what it is to have compassion. Cynthia's face teaches me that I am seen and loved.

I (Tracey) poke at Adele, for I seem so much cooler with 1500+ Facebook friends. We are separated by a few decades, and my generation has sucked up social media like a Shop-Vac. I agree that sitting with a friend like Cynthia is the only way to truly see her, to take in the health of her complexion and pick up that new rattle in her voice, but I find social media opens and expands avenues for meaningful connections. It is a new venue through which to be a friend, and true connection on social media really is possible.

Tragic instances of cyberbullying convey the power social media has for connectivity. If people can so injure one another through social media that depression and even suicide result, can't the reverse be true? We can electronically champion one another, promote one another's work, cheer on old friends, connect with new ones and tell the world about the neighbor we adore whose watercolor is on display this weekend for the first time ever. It feels good to be noticed and encouraged, electronically or in person. Whether we're happy about its prominence or not, technology has broadened avenues for friendship, and it can provide unique, albeit limited, options for connecting at that soul level. Now go friend Adele on Facebook.

NAKED FACES

Our faces—arguably the most vulnerable part of us—go naked into relationships every day. Faces are portals to our souls. They reveal the true you. There are more than forty muscles in the human face, but only five muscles are needed to "survive." Could it be that God gave us all these extra muscles so we learn compassion, empathy and love? What would human survival look like without these qualities? If we don't know the emotions that link us to one another's hearts how can relationships thrive or survive? We need face-to-face interactions to bring out our truest selves.

When I see the melancholy or giggle in your eyes I remember anew that what I do affects you. When I attend to the boring bits of your day (we are all boring sometimes) I grow in patience and understanding. I build connections by watching your face. It is telling that the Hebrew word for face, *panim*, means "presence" or "wholeness of being" as well as a literal face.[4] Being "face to face" with another implies physical, emotional and spiritual presence. God designed the musculature of the human face so that we might be able to express the wholeness of our being and receive the wholeness of another's being. This is the beauty of being face to face.

Genesis contains the story of estranged twin brothers who meet face to face after years apart. The second born, Jacob, was a jerk. He cruelly duped Esau out of his birthright and inheritance. Esau came so unhinged he planned for Jacob's murder. Once Jacob felt the intensity of Esau's rage he disappeared and hid his face from his brother for decades (Genesis 27). Eventually Jacob has to run for his life again and discovers that the only place he can find refuge is back home, but this will mean facing Esau.

In preparation for the encounter Jacob puts all his possessions and family between the two of them. Servants, children, wives, flocks, as well as vast quantities of presents are lined up between Jacob and Esau, out in the field, to sweeten the meeting. Unexpectedly, grace oozes into the story. Hell-bent, once-murderous Esau shows more interest in welcoming the face of Jacob, his dear brother, than in receiving gifts. Jacob, overwhelmed and humbled, blurts out, "To see your face is like seeing the face of God" (Genesis 33:10). There is power in receiving a face. It is a divine pathway toward reconciliation and peace.

In Victor Hugo's *Les Miserables*, Jean Valjean sings, "To love another person is to see the face of God."[5] To be present—face to face—can undo us and remake us. Looking into the eyes of someone who longs to be forgiven and received again can soften us. When the psalmist longs for God he asks to see God's face (Psalm 17:15; 102:2). When Aaron blessed the Hebrew people he said, "The LORD bless you and keep you; the LORD make his face shine on you and be gracious to you; the LORD turn his face toward you and give you peace" (Numbers 6:24-26). Being face to face was the cry of his heart—it is the cry of every heart.

Friendship happens when we are true faced with another. Friendship requires the gift of presence and face. Look around—there are gift faces all around you. Do you want them? The path to friendship requires that we risk engaging with them. Are you holding out for particular faces? Sometimes the friends we long for don't choose us back. Other women may not be in the same place nor have an interest in seeking friendship with us. We can be overrun with anxiety or perhaps depression over the friends we can't make, or we can receive a sister who is choosing us and find out that they are the very face of God to us. To have friends and be a friend I must find the face of God in them, in me.

SHOWING UP

To grow in friendship we must be tyrannical about honoring time and space for relationships to grow. Simple actions like leaving the phone in your car while picking up a child from school or refusing to check it while heading from the parking lot or train to the office allows us vanishing graces—graces like making eye contact or saying a kind word to another woman whom God may have set aside for us as a "friendly face." Unless we are diligent in seeing others we will brush daily past potential connections and flop into bed at night lamenting the lonely ache in our hearts.

There is tension between longings for friendship and the realities of busy lives, yet a UCLA study indicates that if we want to cope well with the tensions in life we need girlfriends. It seems women respond to stress with a larger behavioral repertoire than just fight or flight:

> When the hormone oxytocin is released as part of the stress response in a woman, it buffers the flight or fight response and encourages her to tend children and gather with other women instead. When she actually engages in this tending or be-friending studies suggest that more oxytocin is released, which further counters stress and produces a calming effect. This calming response does not occur in men.[6]

Carol Rinkleib Ellison, a clinical psychologist in private practice in Loomis, California, and former assistant clinical psychiatry professor at the University of California–San Francisco suggests this is an attachment hormone that "creates feelings of calm and closeness."[7]

Our friendships are not the frivolous interruptions to the larger scheme of life that our media often portrays. Instead, they increase our health and the possibility of surviving life's worst. Friendship makes the mundane, celebratory and tragic idiosyncrasies of life more bearable. God is there in the faces of our friends.

For those of us who are married, friends can also fill gaps in our marriages. Avenues to friendship open up when we admit that marriage is not designed to meet our every relational need. My (Adele) husband, Doug, feels relief when girlfriends shore up my word quota for the day. Doug generously encourages me to meet some of my desire for conversation, walks and artistic activities through women friends. He knows that it is not good for either of us if he is the only one I talk to. Nurturing the true you for women who are married involves deep friendships outside of their marriages.

THOSE GOOD INTENTIONS

I (Tracey) have felt drawn to a few women in unique ways. I have felt an instant connection, but often life has moved too fast to allow it to take root. I once told a woman I adored that I believed we would be great friends who tried to change the world together if only we had more time. She instantly agreed and we giggled a bit over the audacious pace of our lives, then dashed back to our grinds, never ultimately connecting. Intention alone will not give us friendship; we must follow through.

When we feel friendless, as we all inevitably will, we find solace in knowing that Jesus actually calls us "friend" (John 15:15). Regardless of the pain-filled snubs of life, we are invited into a divine friendship with Jesus. Being his friend draws us up into the life and belonging of the Trinity, who does the divine life as a Holy Three, who orchestrates life in a group and is in its very essence community. God is the Great Befriender, and the gift of divine friendship reminds us that if Jesus sees us as a friend then, indeed, we are deserving of friends! There is a sisterhood of women of God that reaches back to Eve. These women have laughed, labored and carried burdens together, and we share their story. The haunches of history can whisper encouragements to us in lonely moments. It takes time and intention to link with sisters and develop a band of friends, but God's design for our lives is that we indeed find these connections.

Friendships thrive on proximity, but in our increasingly transient culture we must maximize creative ways to build sisterhood when we are not together. During graduate school Adele was in a small group of six women. They were not a homogenous group that spent all their time together, but they did gather to pray for one another during the week. When they graduated, scattered across the country, they decided to keep in touch through a round-robin letter. This snail-mail missive has traveled between the six of them for nearly forty years (nearly as long as Tracey has been alive). Adele has penned her fears, named her desperation, dumped her longings and vented her frustrations. And each time she removes her old letter from the envelope and reads the five letters inside, she knows that she can trust these women with her life. They have laughed at her foibles, saved her sanity and helped her to remember her true self and to see God in her story.

RUTH AND NAOMI

One of the most exquisitely simple stories in Scripture is the journey of Ruth and Naomi. We confess it feels pretty rote and redundant to land this chapter here. Ruth is the expected text in thousands of women's devotional resources and for good reason. There is perhaps no stronger biblical narrative of female friendship than their shared journey.

This story unfolds primarily through conversation. Fifty out of the eighty-five verses are dialogue. It is really no surprise that this narrative of two women is told through the medium of conversation.

Swirling in grief after the men (Naomi's husband and her two sons) whose livelihood kept the family thriving had all died, three ordinary women are left alone in a world uncharitable to their gender. Their shared journey saves their lives.

Ruth and Naomi's friendship points us to Christ—the One who called us friend and then laid down his life for us. Laying down our lives for our friends is a God-like thing to do. One of the most healing salves for the soul is for someone to say, "I will go there with you." I will go with you through cancer, addiction, the fear-inducing 3:00 a.m. phone call, the divorce or financial ruin. I will be that face of God to you. Ruth and Naomi had limitations, losses and a lack of resources. They could no more guarantee a hope-filled future than we can today, but being together gave them courage, and their trust in Naomi's God gave them hope. Ruth's story reveals God's design for friendship. Two women travel as far as bodies and minds can get them with one another, and they lean into God for the rest. This is the essence of sisterhood.

Some friends take the place of family. They are soul friends, coursing through our lives with more love and grace than our own flesh and blood. Like Ruth and Naomi we are bound to them forever. These friends invite us into the Trinity. We come together and share the bloodline of the God who has been Father and Mother to us. We are not only friends in the flesh but sisters in the Spirit. To quote my friend Julie, "Some friends go way back. Spiritual friends go way deep." We journey together into the sacred and the ridiculous—our hearts leaning together in the love of God. In this womb of love and trust we grow up.

God has created us to experience this depth and meaning in our friendships. If you find yourself reading this, utterly alone, shaking your head in anger, please know that *you* can experience friendship like this. It may not be at this very moment, but the very God of the universe designed you to give and receive it, for the sake of the true you. Do not lose hope.

JOURNAL AND PRACTICE

The topic of friendship can dredge up past hurts or nostalgia for what once was. Perhaps you long for a companion like Ruth or Naomi. Perhaps you find yourself smiling at the fact that you have a person like this in your life. No matter what you feel, conversations on friendship give us reasons to pray through our stories.

1. In John 15:15, Jesus calls his disciples "friends." Can you hear Jesus call you "friend"? Begin your prayers this week by addressing God as "Dear Friend." Let God befriend you in those tender places where longing and desire for companionship live.

2. Make a list of the places you belong and how this belonging addresses any loneliness in your soul. Where do these belongings fill you with gratitude? This week notice your places of belonging and thank God in the moment.

3. Celebrate the good and trustworthy characteristics you notice in other women, even a stranger or acquaintance. Compliment them. Become present to qualities that might make them a valuable friend for you or another woman. This simple act of becoming aware affirms and celebrates our sisterhood and helps you recognize qualities you are drawn to in friendships. What sort of women are you drawn to? Why?

4. When we recognize the goodness in others we may see ways in which we long to become better friends to others. Risk asking a friend, "I want to be a better friend to you. What are ways I can change and grow in our relationship?"

5. Write the story of a friendship journey that has shaped you (positive or negative). What were the joys or aches of that relationship? How has that friendship changed you and your journey with God?

6. Who taught you the art of friendship (whether positive or negative aspects)? What did you learn from them? What do you know about yourself as a friend?

7. For those who lead, pastor or coach other women, what might you do differently (or be sure to continue doing) when you consider women's needs for friendship? Is there a place in your workplace, church, school, ministry or teaching to address the story of Ruth and Naomi again?

3

COMPETITORS
OR COMRADES

I mistook her for my enemy.

DALE HANSON BOURKE

❦

A few years ago we had an opening for the executive pastor position at the church where I (Tracey) serve. It's a big congregation, so this was a high-level role that included preaching and teaching, managing large teams and maintaining a public ministry profile. We were excited to see who might fill this position, yet I panicked the day I learned one of the final candidates was a woman.

As the only female on our pastoral staff you would think I'd be elated, thrilled to have an injection of estrogen into the all-male executive leadership. Perhaps I might even bang on the doors of our personnel committee making a case for evening out the leadership ranks. After all, statistically women occupy slightly more than 50 percent of the pew space in American churches today. Why not insist the leadership reflect the congregation?

Instead I felt threatened. It took me a few days to name it. The tiny drop of enthusiasm I had diluted into a bucket of fear, jealousy, comparison and competition. What if we only had room for one woman on our staff? Would her coming diminish my contribution? I was the token girl pastor!

To be fair, I serve a gracious senior pastor who supports and encourages male and female staff alike. But I still panicked. Would I still get to preach and teach? Or would I have to level her in the hallway so that I could keep leading? Would we be comrades or competitors?

COMPETITIVE SPIRIT

A fear like this is not unique. It is, in part, driven by a culture that believes there are only so many slices in the proverbial pie. Who doesn't want to be somebody when life at the bottom of the food chain is risky? We have deep roots in broken economic and social theories that operate under the assumption that for one person to ascend to leadership or economic success another must fall. There is only so much financial wealth, only so many As to be awarded on the curve, only so many chairs in the boardroom. Competition can certainly be a good thing. It is one way best practices and ideas rise to the top. But it can also injure our true you when we are threatened, or we want to tidy or savvy ourselves up a bit, perhaps even fake another out, in order to win.

I (Adele) was surprised by Tracey's perspective because I've worked with her and never experienced it as competition. In fact, true to the stereotype, I've found men to be more competitive than women. The women I've worked with have been less confrontational, more collaborative and harder to read than men.

Tracey owns her competitive streak. She's sitting here in my study all energized about how much she loves to win and totally confounded that at times I'll give up and refuse to play the game. She can't refuse a game. I've worked in settings where it's no compliment to be considered ambitious, outspoken and assertive, so I compete more with myself than with others. I do not want to alienate or be dismissed as that hyperdriven, hard-as-nails, know-it-all woman.

Tracey doesn't let it drop. She asks, "Is that the only reason you don't want to compete?"

I mutter, "Well, maybe I'm afraid to fail."

Sheryl Sandberg writes, "Fear is at the root of so many of the barriers that women face. Fear of not being liked. Fear of making the wrong choice. Fear of drawing negative attention. Fear of overreaching. Fear of being judged. Fear of failure. And the holy trinity of fear: the fear of being a bad mother/wife/daughter."[1]

Our friend Julie Baier lists a fourth fear:

> Sometimes when I've chosen not to join in competition it's because I've actually feared winning. In my experience, winners can sometimes be despised because they're perceived as a threat. I've even been known to dumb myself down in order to be perceived as less competitive and more palatable to those I love. It is this deeper need of my heart for love and acceptance that drives my energy to compete or not and, I've found, it's essential that I'm able to name and own it.

Fear of "winning" can also mask our true you.

WHAT THEY ARE SAYING

The National Bureau of Economic Research ran a study that suggests, "When it comes to competitiveness, women just don't stack up."[2] According to the World Economic Forum's annual report, in every single country where data exists women earn less than men in similar jobs. The reasons for this abound, but in part, women tend to shy away from competition where men engage with it.[3]

ABC News reports a study involving nearly seven thousand job seekers in sixteen large American cities, "Women shy away from competitive workplaces whereas men covet, and even thrive in, competitive environments." The results of the study suggest that men are more likely than women to apply for positions where success is based on competition or commission. Women are more likely to apply for positions with flat salaries and the promise of working with a team.[4] *Upstart Business Journal* also suggests most women join companies to be part of a team. They often indicate, more than men, that they want to relate to coworkers, clients and vendors as friends.[5]

Yet none of this research reveals the full story on competition. How does competition encourage or squelch the true you?

WHAT'S WITH THE WOMEN WHO DO COMPETE?

People lean into or shy away from competition for a variety of deeper heart desires. For some, winning is simply a rush. They love the thrill, the training and the team work it takes to achieve. It brings out good elements of their true selves. Yet competition can foster a menacing dark side, stemming from insecurity.

Some want to prove they are special or knowledgeable. It can feel good to win at work or in a volunteer setting when the truth about other parts of life is that they seem like places we always lose. Perhaps success eludes us in our careers, academics or marriages, but we can Pottery Barn our apartment or home to the envy of all our friends. They wish they lived like us. This competitive streak comes from a tainted, broken place. It's not operating out of the truest you.

We can compete about anything from being the most loving to the most gregarious, to having the most dramatic life. It's not whether or not we compete but why we compete that reveals what is going on beneath the thin veneer of our lives.

Tracey's reaction to the potential church hire was based in a very rational experience: female staff positions at churches are rare and many times nonexistent. The stats on female staff fuel anxiety that can drive competition. Whether because of valid professional panic or nagging insecurities, we often pit ourselves against one another. Rather than look with joy and celebration at the accomplishments of another woman we compare:

- So . . . where did you go on vacation?
- You just got a tech job in XYZ hip city?
- Oh, so your child just applied to college where?
- They got another new car?!
- Gosh, her pumps are Louboutin?
- Where do you work?

Women compare their grades, friends, kids, first jobs, fiancés, daughters' weddings. We compare chest size, hair, double chins and who's skinny enough to rock their skinny jeans. The two of us confess we have already stacked ourselves up against half the authors we know. There are a lot of good books out there, and people don't have a ton of time to read. What will our Amazon ranking be?

Many women who have achieved even the most minute seniority agree that their biggest challenges stem from other women. The most devastating hate mail we both have received came from women. We know the archetypal tales of the male glass ceiling that can keep us down, but the reality is that estrogen can also do you in. Significant roadblocks in both leadership and life can come from sisters. There are many reasons we diminish one another's voices and positions. They may be pretty, rich, thin, smart, accomplished, take your pick. Women can cast long shadows. Rather than having each other's backs, we have a thumb and forefinger around the throat. Irish novelist Edna O'Brien is credited with saying, "I have some women friends but I prefer men. Don't trust women. There is a built-in competition between women."

BULLYING

A social worker friend in a large suburban high school says, "Girls bullying girls is hands down one of the most substantial adolescent issues I deal with." She laments that girls often terrorize one another for sport. Where did we learn this? We know how harrowing this feels, so why do we keep it up after high school? Grown women devour one another for a spot in the Junior League, a seat at the speaker's table or an invitation to the big event that *everyone* wanted. And brace yourself, the pictures will be posted on Facebook to taunt you with the fact that you weren't there.

We've heard dozens of stories about girls and women using their strength and position to intimidate others. Online bullying or verbal, physical or emotional intimidation have disabled women we love. Bullies often act out of places of deep pain, feelings of inadequacy and insecurity. An inability to win at some form of competition (for love, affection, parental attention, etc.) keeps some in a cycle of injuring others. On the flip side, when we feel solidarity or union with others we don't power up; instead, we see others as being on the same team, allies.

Amy Di Santo has been a soccer coach at both Dana Hall School and Dover-Sherborn High School in Massachusetts. She tries to teach her team that they each have a unique purpose, so they aren't competing for the same slot. She tells them, "Think about all the people who had to come together to make you. Trace your ancestry back. If one person was missing you wouldn't be here." Arriving at the true you means letting go of fears and comparisons and the need to aggressively seek your own advantage. It means remembering that what is truest and best about us might come out when we cooperate and work as a team rather than compete to be the lone star.

PSALM 139

God reminds us in Psalm 139 that we all have value and meaning:

> For you created my inmost being;
> you knit me together in my mother's womb.
> I praise you because I am fearfully and wonderfully made;
>   your works are wonderful, I know that full well.
> My frame was not hidden from you
>   when I was made in the secret place,

when I was woven together in the depths of the earth.
Your eyes saw my unformed body;
all the days ordained for me were written in your book
before one of them came to be.
How precious to me are your thoughts, God!
How vast is the sum of them!
Were I to count them,
they would outnumber the grains of sand—
when I awake, I am still with you.

Your being here means you have a particular purpose that is unique to you. No other person can accomplish your purpose no matter how hard they compete. And you cannot accomplish theirs, even if it does look better, smarter, sexier or easier. Your purpose belongs to you! Can you feel the freedom in this? Do you really want to spend your energies chasing someone else's purpose rather than realizing your own?

Seeing your own unique place in the world allows you to see others as gifted, necessary contributors. Trusting that they have a unique purpose themselves opens our eyes to their true you. Romans 12 reminds us that we are all part of the body of Christ and are therefore highly valued, loved and essential. The reality of how God sees people can move us to encourage even those we don't particularly like in their purpose. Imagine what sort of world we could create if we moved from being against others to being on their side and having their back.

Comparison can rob us of confidence and spiral into self-loathing. It destroys the glue between people and can create bully behavior. If who you are has suddenly become so much bigger, so much more fantastic than I am, I lose track of my own belovedness and my own connection to you as a sister. I begin a narrative. You may not even know I'm comparing myself to you. Heck, I may not even know you! But this narrative has power to impact how I relate to you, myself and

God. I look at you with your success and your gorgeous head of hair, and suddenly I'm angry with you and with God.

ENOUGH TO GO AROUND?

God did not create the world out of deficit and divine need. God created out of abundant fullness and love. Creation swarms, teems and overflows with goodness and life. Even God's first command, to be fruitful and multiply, speaks to the Creator's desire to have abundance everywhere. Comparison undermines the awareness of God's abundance. We start to believe God has favorites and we are not one of them. *Why does she have so many friends? Why do her kids get every break? Why did she get to travel like that? Why can she turn so many heads? Why did she get the great marriage?*

Do you see what has happened? Competition and comparison have turned a world of abundance into a world of scarcity. The narrative has expanded just enough to include a stingy God. While we may think those at the top of the pile experience more of God's happiness, favoritism and love, they can also struggle with a famished narrative. Are they loved for who they are or what they can do for you? Is this the reason for the cliché, "It's lonely at the top"?

Where does the scarcity narrative trip up your true you? All day long God was present to the people of Israel in a cloud. At night God's presence was visible in a pillar of fire. God was with them—in both very tangible symbols and in their experience. Yet the whole Exodus story is riddled with scarcity. Will there be enough water, meat, comfort, protection? Will this God they follow ever be enough to replace what they had before they left their comforts and traveled the desert?

The Israelites' fixation on scarcity warped the narrative. They forgot that God pulled them up from the rigors of slavery. They forgot the Red Sea. But they remembered the savory meat, the leeks, the garlic of Egypt. "Can't we go back?!" Even God's miracle of ambrosial manna could not compare. When set against the full bellies of Egypt they turned the good God had given into no good at all. We do this, yes? Haven't we turned the good of our own bodies or lives into no good at all? Or the gift of our voice and wisdom somehow stays silent because we fear it is not as savvy as another?

Our Exodus stories only move from scarcity to abundance when we own that not getting what we want doesn't mean that God checked out on us. We are still beloved, "the apple of God's eye" (Psalm 17:8; Zechariah 2:8). There is no need to compete for belovedness. There is enough of God and goodness to go around—even on a day with my bank account at zero and a parking ticket on my window.

When I trust that God sees me with the same abundant love that is there for you it is harder to perceive you as a threat. It is easier to embrace your true you because it is not a threat to me. We are both held together in God's heart. And if I am in union with you in God's heart then why wouldn't I share rather than compete? I too have gifts and one unrepeatable life in this amazing world. While it might not look like yours, in Christ it matters just the same. God sees us both through eyes of abundant love. God wants the best for both of us. That is the gospel truth. Rather than estranged siblings arguing over how to divide an inheritance, we are sisters, sitting at the same table. We are here to cheer one another on.

As author C. Joybell C. once noted,

> I just believe that us as women—should not criticize nor pull down other women. And why? Because we're all just trying our best to be beautiful! We all just want to be loved, . . . we're all trying to leave our own legacy! So why spend even a second on trying to take away from another woman? Trying to steal, trying to criticize, trying to oppress? . . . When you waste any amount of time trying to take what is another's—you are wasting your huge chunk of a galaxy that's already been given to you!"[6]

Think of all the collective energy we waste on comparing and snarking. If by the grace of God this energy could be unleashed in the direction of love—if we could love our sisters as ourselves—we would watch the Kingdom come. "Your kingdom come. Your will be done. On earth as it is in heaven."

JOURNAL AND PRACTICE

1. Tracey doesn't like this practice, but she is going to do it anyway. Practice playing some games for the fun of it rather than the rush of the win. Can you help make the game fun for others? Encourage your competitor. Talk or journal about what it is like for you.

2. If you shy away from the challenge of competition, begin to notice where you are not taking responsibility for the gifts you have been given. Where do you need to say, "I know something about that. Perhaps even more than you. So I am happy to take the lead."

3. Find someone to promote and believe in other than yourself. Give away some authority and consider what that feels like for you. Collaborate. Encourage. Work for a win-win rather than a solo victory, even if a solo victory may seem initially easier.

4. Identify a person with whom you constantly compare yourself. Make two columns, one that represents everything you think she has that you are lacking, the other for everything God has given you. What is God showing you when you see these things?

5. Make a list of a few competitive efforts and collaborative efforts. Write about the results of each effort. What satisfaction (long or short term) did it bring you? What do you become aware of?

6. Write about what it is like to celebrate someone else's success and cheer on a person who, for one reason or another, threatens you. In your journal write a congratulatory note to them.

7. When you lose a client, a game, a promotion, a sale, a position, etc., how do you spin what happened so you still look like a success? What good could come from being authentic about your failures?

4

CALL THE MIDWIFE!

When I might otherwise go under.

KAREN PURCELL

I (Tracey) sat one evening at our kitchen table and watched as my son tangled his index fingers through his hair, grabbed a fistful of curls and yanked. Then he shoved his math homework at me and hollered through his tears, "I must be stupid!"

It was fourth-grade homework, not the ACT, or a job interview or the chance to cure cancer, but he was inhabiting the lead in his own tragedy. I was fighting my urge to roar back, "Pull yourself together! It's only freaking homework!" With a pointed finger I slid the paper back. "Let's walk through this again." More tears. The answers were obvious to me, but my son had to discover them on his own. I was there to bring grace. My job was to stay with him at the table until he finished—long after his siblings trotted off to play. It was on me to help bolster his confidence so he could complete an assignment and grow in some emotional maturity. We often need this same support in our lives, a friend, mentor, pastor, parent or leader who sits beside us and helps us stay true to ourselves in the depths of tragedy or as new opportunities emerge in our lives.

LABOR

This is how so many beautiful moments of life and the soul are birthed. Someone sits beside us with a different perspective or a calmer heart, and they help us push our way into new life. (I know not all of us are moms who have given birth—yet here comes a birth story, so stick with me.) The midwife who helped deliver my firstborn met us at the hospital not with medical supplies but with her knitting. Her knitting! As I howled and paced and labored—for hours!—she sat in the corner in a rocking chair with her needles and yarn. "Really? You're knitting? Because I'm pretty much having a baby."

"Let me know when you need me. This is your labor," she whispered as her needles clacked away. "Consider walking like this. Or maybe stand this way."

Here were firm suggestions from decades of experience. I could take or leave them. When the groans, ripping and tearing of birth began, the yarn went back in the bag. Her gentle suggestions became orders as my husband and I looked to her in terror. She took command and met us in the panic, yet it was me having the baby. She could take me only so far.

A midwife labors with you, not for you. She settles you into solidarity with thousands upon thousands of women who have labored before you. Midwives trust what a woman's body can do, but they know each body has limits. Her presence is to help you find your strength in suffering. We all, whether we ever give birth or not, need other women to help call up our strength when we lose it (or never even knew we had it). We can all use friends who understand how to be there as midwives as we give birth to our true you—not just once but over and over again.

SPIRITUAL MIDWIFERY

Our souls ache for others who will midwife us into confidence, depth, acceptance and emotional maturity. Who will bring us to our true you? We need partners to birth wisdom beyond our experiences, kindness beyond our feelings, patience beyond our urge to control, trust beyond fear and love beyond self.

Jesus said, "The Advocate, the Holy Spirit, whom the Father will send in my name, will teach you all things and will remind you of everything I have said to you. Peace I leave with you; my peace I give you. I do not give to you as the world gives. Do not let your hearts be troubled and do not be afraid" (John 14:25-27). The Spirit's fruit of love, joy, peace, forbearance, kindness, goodness, faithfulness, gentleness and self-control doesn't come automatically. It comes through travail. It is nurtured in the womb of suffering, and one of the roles of the Holy Spirit is to midwife us as we bear the fruit of God in our lives. The Spirit labors with us and tarries with us and broods over the dark, deep places to get us through the storms and into the arms of Jesus. But this often happens in partnership with others. When we invite another woman to help carry our pain, we have also invited the peace of God to touch us through her. God often comes to us through the presence of others—others committed to seeing and rejoicing in the birth of our true selves.

Emilie Griffin puts it like this,

> What has been nurtured in Mary's womb is our fertility. Mary labors to give birth to the Christ who rules in us. We are somehow the womb, the creative environment in which Christ's meaning can take hold, be nourished in dark places, grow and swell, breaking open at last in ways that can heal and invigorate our lives. We ourselves, who are powerless, we who are spiritually and materially needy, we who know the pinch of want, we also know the Lord's generosity to us.[1]

All the feminine metaphors so easily skimmed over (womb, midwife, labor, birthing) reflect deep spiritual realities of how we are transformed in partnership with the Holy Spirit and others.

PAIN

Nurse midwives assure a woman in labor that she will forget the pain once the baby comes. One dared tell me I was feeling "pressure" more than pain. But she was actually on to something. Time and again intense pressure precedes something new. Looking back I have evidence there were places in my soul that didn't exist until pain crashed in and delivered them. I don't want to ever relive that pain, but I am grateful for the empathy, understanding and compassion that emerged out of mire and tears. Left to my own pursuit of comfort these safe places in my soul would never have been birthed in me.

Mother Teresa is believed to have said, "I have found the paradox, that if you love until it hurts, there can be no more hurt, only more love." I would choke on these words were they not from her. She lived her every word, and look what it birthed. All the justice, art and beauty of her life came from laboring with others who were in pain. God does not intend for us to face pain alone. We are called the body of Christ for a reason. Smash your thumb and the whole body will launch a rescue.

We labor with others so that both sides can deepen their true selves. This idea of laboring with another does not mean we can absolve and erase pain. When Adele's pain got to be too much in labor, she flat out refused to push—she was over it. The midwife let Adele know she could lie on the table and argue or she could push that baby out. But then the midwife put her hands on Adele's abdomen and helped her push. She gave her strength to do it.

Midwifing is not always about getting women through a delivery. Tracey has been riding shotgun with a friend in the thick of a nearly impossible situation. Ultimately her friend is the one who must move, stand before a judge, pony up the cash to rally the lawyers and begin a new life. Tracey cannot actually do any of these things for her friend. It's not on us to eradicate another woman's pain or fully absorb her burden. In the end, only God can take on that one. Our responsibility is to prop up our sisters and enter as far into the mess as they invite us to go. We put a shoulder to their load and give our presence to their pain so they know they are not alone. Sometimes that simple fact is everything.

Paul gives some guidelines on how we can carry our own stuff and schlep someone else's at the same time. "Shoulder each other's burdens, and then you will live as the law of the Anointed teaches us. . . . Each person has his or her own burden to bear and story to write" (Galatians 6:2, 5, The Voice). The Greek word for "burden" in verse two is *baros*, which means "weight, heaviness, trouble."[2] *Baros* carries the sense of a crushing load too big for anyone to manage alone. In verse five, the Greek word for burden is *phortion*, which points to the weight of a backpack a soldier must carry.[3] This suggests a load that we can carry alone.

Life comes with *baros* burdens and catastrophes that overwhelm and slam us down. When a sister redistributes the *baros*, that weight shifts, and perhaps we can stand upright again, no longer hopelessly squashed by the weight.

Even so, everyone shoulders their own backpack (*phortion*) of unique misunderstandings, disappointments, criticisms, broken relationships, etc. These things are stapled to us and we can't dish them out. Paul indicates that since they are ours to transport through this life we need both Jesus' grace and presence within the community and within us to carry the load. Sometimes, we need to haul our own load. Other times, we get help. Watch Jesus: when he felt crushed by the path to the cross, he said to his disciples, "My soul is overwhelmed with sorrow to the point of death. Stay here and keep watch" (Mark 14:34). Jesus shared his *baros* with them; even when they failed to come through, they were his friends. But, the *phortion* was his alone to bear. Our *phortions* are part of what make up the "true you" in each of us. They are the realities only we face.

SUFFERING IN SILENCE

So why, then, do we suffer in silence, when clearly we are invited to share our burdens? Why do we end up telling others about our crisis after it is over? Why the pleasantries when our insides feel rubbed raw? What parts of life really should be held in privacy? Not everything is for Instagram and public consumption. Posting every detail or need and baring every privacy can actually scare people away. Yet is hiding the fact that we struggle the solution? Undoubtedly, not everyone is safe to leak on, but feigned perfection and happiness is the utter opposite of the true you.

Some things can be left unsaid, but our tendency is to leave *everything* unsaid. We camouflage ourselves in the midst of people who want to care. Our culture posts everything from being out of milk to how late we were out. But we don't "out" the truth. We put on a persona and strain under our burdens alone. Struggling alone seems the acceptable thing to do. Yet when we discover after the fact how a person we love has suffered in silence, we are confounded and all achy inside. To us, their friends, their people, it so injures the heart to know they suffered alone.

Daring to answer the "How are you?" greeting with more than a rote "great" puts us at risk. Some people don't want a real answer; they don't have time or capacity to engage. Flat-out rejection is so painful that most of us would rather struggle alone than risk handing our true you to someone who can't receive it.

Jesus risked handing his fear to his friends. He risked appearing needy and overwhelmed. He risked letting them into his delivery room of pain—where he gave birth to "not my will but [God's] be done." Jesus' risk meant that his disciples could let him down and that betrayal could be next. You and I know that Jesus' friends did let him down, and Jesus had to do the work in his pain alone. But he never stopped risking that God was good and that something new could be birthed out of his suffering: life out of death, joy out of sorrow, hope out of desolation.

Vulnerability can birth something in us. If you let me down I can enter the pain that gives birth to forgiveness and you can enter the pain that gives birth to repentance. Brene Brown says, "Embracing our vulnerabilities is risky but not nearly as dangerous as giving up on love and belonging and joy—the experiences that make us the most vulnerable."[4] Let someone safe into the pain-filled rooms of your life. Risk that something good can come from not going it alone.

BEYOND PAIN

What needs to be birthed in you? Who will help you deliver it? Midwifing often happens when tragedy strikes and the need is immediate. In the moment of triage, often all that is needed is a prayerful presence, someone who is with you as you labor. As things unfold we will need a midwife who can see what needs to be birthed in us: learning to risk on God, how to move toward forgiveness, how to let go of pain and not become bitter, how to find (or recover) our own strength. A good midwife won't push us faster than we can go.

We also need sisters to help tease the good and beautiful out of our lives in the ordinary humdrum. We need women who can point out an untapped gift or unearth a repressed passion. Mentors, teachers or friends, who can listen closely to our stories with an ear to what makes us anxious or excited, help us discover gifts and callings we may otherwise miss.

The midwifing of others lifted me (Tracey) up off the floor during the anger and tears of marital skirmishes. Midwives gave me strength to navigate deep caverns of grief after losing a bosom friend. I'm not completely paralyzed in parenting my children, because other moms tell me their stories and wisdom. Neither one of us would be on our current professional paths were it not for midwives who saw a future we could not see.

When my (Adele's) kids were young, a friend midwifed my parenting as well. She was fifteen years older, and she was able to say true things like: "Adele, you did this all wrong." Again and again she rescued my children from my overserious self. During my thirteen years in Chicagoland I met monthly with a group of six women all gifted in soul midwifery. They walked me through crises that could have pulled me under, and taught me what it looked like to be emotionally healthy and present to God. They taught me that pain that is not transformed is transmitted. They showed me how to bear a bruise rather than become calloused. A bruised heart can still be touched.

WHAT GOD DOES WITH PAIN

Pain is not the worst thing that can happen to us. In fact, the worst day in history happened to Jesus—and we know that it became the best day. God is in and can transform tragedy. The psalmist sings, "You turned my wailing into dancing; you removed my sackcloth and clothed me with joy, that my heart may sing your praises and not be silent. LORD my God, I will praise you forever!" (Psalm 30:11-12). Trust is not some sort of divine denial. God does not erase the past with its pain, but the story about our pain changes. God tells the Israelites to remember their history as slaves in Egypt but that slavery is not to define them since God rescued them and set them free. Our pain does not have to define us. "Weeping may stay for the night, but rejoicing comes in the morning" (Psalm 30:5).

Each one of us is a potential midwife. Some of us feel like a broken pile of bones waiting to be cast and set; we feel we can't face the pain in another's story. That's okay—your turn will come. Others have the energy, time and extra grace to come alongside and help time the contractions. Mostly, though, we are not afforded the luxury of deciding if, when and how to help. Life happens. One phone call or text is all it takes to find ourselves in that birthing room, waiting to catch someone else's baby.

Midwifery always begins with presence. It is being in the moment with what is. What is happening in the lives of people around you?

Are you so distracted that you are blind to what you could give right now? Could you mentor, coach or befriend? A good midwife creates a circle of trust and love around the birth. One day we are the mentor, coach or befriender and the next day the roles shift and we hope to land in the capable hands of therapists, spiritual directors and friends. Think about your own circles and who is present to you. Can you create a circle of love and trust? The faces in that circle will at times confound you. It is not always the ones we expect who walk with us and help carry our load.

We can see God's midwifing of us in the Greek word for "salvation," which is linked to the root *sōzō*. It means "to keep safe," "to save a suffering one from perishing," "to make well or heal," "to restore to health one who is suffering." When we say that Jesus came to save us, it means that Jesus came to restore us to whole life: body, mind and spirit. Salvation is the process of a lifetime with a promise that, in the end, all tears will be wiped away, all wounds will be sacred wounds (like Jesus hands and feet), and God will birth our truest and most beautiful self.

JOURNAL AND PRACTICE

1. Have a gathering that celebrates "midwifing." Invite some friends to bring an object with them that symbolizes something God has birthed in them through a time of pain and suffering. After each woman shares, honor her journey with prayers of thanksgiving. Honor the God that can bring good things out of "bad" parts of our stories.

2. Tell the story of someone you know who has been full of love even though her life came with suffering. How is she different from other people? What does she see that others often miss? Are there people who are ready to hear this story? When you see someone in "labor," remember this story and pray for them.

3. Make a timeline of the big heartaches, sorrows and losses in your life. Beneath each event draw a picture of the fruit or distortion that was born in the furnace of this pain: anger, bitterness, distrust, hope, perseverance, compassion, acceptance, etc. What do you want to tell God about what you see in your life? Looking back, what do you see about God's presence that you couldn't see at the time?

4. Read a biography about someone who has grown into an amazing person through trials and storms. Consider *Unbroken* by Laura Hillenbrand or *I Heard the Owl Call My Name* by Margaret Craven.

5. Hurts can be so devastating that we bury them and try to forget. The truth is our bodies and subconscious remember. We may have recurring dreams or behaviors that are riddled with fear. Consider journaling to recover your story. (Don't be afraid to check in with a therapist if you need to. Then tackle your journal.) Ask God to help you sift through a painful chapter, looking for the moments where the Holy Spirit was present to midwife a new beginning. Reclaim all the parts of your story. They make you who you are.

6. Suffering can reveal what matters most in life. Imagine you have a year to live. Write about what you would do. What would receive your time and energies? How does knowing what you would do influence the way you live your story now?

7. What does your circle of love and trust look like? Who is in it? Who may need you, and who do you need? Notice if someone specific is being given to you at this moment. What can you do for her? How can you walk with her?

PART TWO

True Life

5

SHINY OBJECTS

Can't stop now. Won't miss out.

ADELE CALHOUN AND
TRACEY BIANCHI

I (Tracey) recently upgraded my phone. I'm a sucker for technology. My old model was slow and dodgy, cracked across the back, and tacky with fingerprints and sweat marks from grabby little hands. When I slid open the slick packaging on the new version I marveled at the fresh electronic canvas, not a fingerprint on the touch screen. I made a vow: I promised not to drop this one or load it up with so many apps that I couldn't find my calendar.

This phone was clean, uncluttered, filled with the potential to probably launch a rocket. It calmed me. I feel the same way about blank legal pads and brand-new #2 pencils. Our lives start like this—fresh out of the box, blank screens and pages, and space for apps and downloads. God created us full of potential. There are places to go, things to do and people to see. Over time, though, we download an app store's worth of needless items, big files that drag on us, and our operating systems no longer respond with a click. We lament that it takes forever to download anything.

As a child you arrived in life free and unencumbered, given to fits of creativity and play. It's when we age that the clutter kicks in—class schedules, tuition, marriage, mortgage, divorce, second mortgage, debt. Keeping up and keeping on. The apps open too slowly. *What was it I was trying to do again?* When our lives fill with burden and fear it takes a million clicks to get to our true identity. Easing up on our fears of missing out will keep our souls freed up and keep us in touch with our truest selves.

FEAR OF MISSING OUT

Adele meets regularly with some Ivy League chaplains who confide in each other about the thinness of their souls and the keyed up, fragmented, never-done nature of their lives. They lament that their campus cultures are competitive, entitled, consumeristic and driven. No one has healthy boundaries. You have to push yourself. Go everywhere. Meet everyone. Do everything. If you aren't where it's happening, you're no one. This ethos has a name. It's called FOMO (fear of missing out). FOMO is fueled by a need to have the most exhilarating, accomplished story.

You don't have to be an Ivy League gal to struggle with FOMO. The twenty-first century sets you up for frenetic, fragmented living. When someone asks, "How are you doing?" it's commonplace to lament: "Sooooooo busy," "Just trying to keep up," "Spinning plates and juggling balls." Have you ever heard a woman say, "I'm taking life slow and feeling like things are manageable"?

Christmas shopping starts in October. Work travel means being away four days this week. On Saturday we have the SAT, three soccer games and a retirement party. We've pressed the fast-forward button. When "free" time presents itself we can't enjoy it anyway. We fidget and fret over how we can never get things done. When we are driven by FOMO we end up jamming our lives full of activities and tasks that give no space for the true you to emerge. Even though we rush, we are stuck in some sort of slow download mode that keeps the true you from coming online.

Our lives are dizzy, and our lists never get shorter. Maybe we don't want them to. Tracey juggles raising three children and a career. Adele thinks (as a Medicare member) that she ought to be slowing down, but life seems as full as ever. Pastoring, writing, speaking, giving spiritual direction, mentoring, being adjunct faculty at various venues and keeping the refrigerator full—it all adds up fast. And then there are friends, families, neighbors. We both have professions that traffic in God and words, but we often can't figure out how to string coherent sentences together. We rely on adrenaline rather than God to get us through. We push into the future without being present to what is. Maybe we have FOMO.

On our better days we consider taking naps, savoring our meals and going to bed early. Adele will go to her studio and paint. Tracey will get out for a run. Still, the sheer velocity and momentum of life is constantly there to sabotage our efforts. We lie down only to have our minds take off, and suddenly it's 2:00 a.m. *Why can't I fall asleep?* Exhaustion, fragmented living and the tyranny of the urgent shadows over the true you of nearly everyone we know.

IF . . . THEN . . .

Do you ever think, "My life won't always be this busy. Any day now I'll get everything under control. I'll finish the to-do list. *Then* I'll slow down and set some limits. *Then* I'll have time for me. *Then* I'll do silence, prayer and thank you cards."

When I say this to Adele, she says, "Dream on, sister. Each season replaces one to-do list with another that is often longer and even more demanding." She tells me the "any day now" thing is a myth. I can dream of the day I slash my schedule, get up an hour earlier, make it to yoga and have time to make really good risotto—the day I become disciplined once and for all. But sooner or later to-do-list momentum pulls me in with my impossibly high expectations and fear of missing out.

"Getting life under control" is a myth awash in so many resolutions and unrealistic expectations. *Did I not try hard enough? Am I not capable enough to pull this off?* Our lives are awash in toxic availability; life without limits or margins; organizing ourselves or our kids for fame, fortune and Harvard; keeping up with those Joneses, and then the Millers, Bergs and Smiths too.

Technology can compound FOMO. It is so easy to click on videos and links that illuminate even more ways we have missed out and been sidelined. The true you gets suffocated in grief and fear over what has been missed. Part of the problem is that we try to have it all without ever defining what "all" is. If we stopped to define it, would we actually want it?

The stress of trying to have it all can literally change our brains. Psychologists say stress impacts how our brains process what's happening. Normal responses to stress are fight, flight or freeze—and when these become our default responses, complex emotions like empathy and compassion don't come online. We can bump into scores of people every day and be so stressed about getting to the next thing that we don't even speak a kind word. In fact, we can't, because we aren't present to anything but our stress.

The cliché is true. The only time we have for living is the present—this moment. In this moment, you can't finish your to-do list. So we begin to manage our FOMO in simple, small ways. Right now, this very instant, you can't get your kid out of trouble or solve their relational issues. Right now you can't fix your resume, colleagues or relationships with your friends and family.

Set down what is not in this moment. Now is not a crack between the present and the future. Now is being present in the Presence. It is being where you are with full attention and intention. Dividing our attention makes us not present to anyone. Twenty-eight hundred years ago the prophet Isaiah said something that sounds completely twenty-first century to me. He wrote, "You have seen many things, but you pay no attention; your ears are open, but you do not listen" (Isaiah 42:20). Whoops! We see life and don't take it in. Our ears are open, but we never stop to ponder what anything means.

TECH LIMITS?

The digital world isso valuable. I (Adele) get to Skype with my son and daughter-in-love in Africa because of this digital world. Tracey works with friends and colleagues without leaving home. Yet when electronics marry our rapid-paced lives, one of two things will happen: either time-saving devices and opportunities will ease our lives, or we will suddenly have distractions that take us across the world with a click and leave behind our much-needed presence in the now. These advances were designed to facilitate connections, but we did not foresee the downside. The temptation in technology is to transfer intimate personal details without honoring the need for emotional presence. We phone when we know people won't pick up. We end a relationship with a text. We Instagram Christmas to others but never engage in the present.

A dear friend discovered her daughter was pregnant via Facebook. The phone call with the news came days later. Her daughter said it was just easier to throw it out there. When breadth and volume replace face-to-face connections, the true you can vanish in the process.

Twenty years of technology has helped us get more done, but it has not fostered greater connectedness. A cover story for *The Atlantic* asks, "Is Facebook Making Us Lonely?" According to Stephen Marche, "In 1985, only 10 percent of Americans said they had no one with whom to discuss important matters. By 2004, 25 percent had nobody to talk to." The article details "the epidemic of loneliness" and how it affects "not only the brain, but the basic process of DNA transcription. When you are lonely, your whole body is lonely."[1] Loneliness infects all the way to our DNA. According to the article, people who write to their friends semiprivately on Facebook are less lonely than those who simply scan friends' status updates and photos but do not engage. It is possible to experience connection via social media, and many among us have profound connections there. But ultimately we need to interact in person to combat loneliness—with a vulnerable and human presence that can hug us, touch us and sense our presence. This form of intimacy comes with limits, though, and it will mean missing out on knowing everybody. Honoring the true you means recognizing the limits of technology and media as well as the way true intimacy limits the time we have for other pursuits.

LIVING WITH LIMITS

God did not design us for flight, yet there is a reckless niche sport called wingsuit flying that refuses to accept this limit. Wingsuit flying makes BASE jumping look like Duck Duck Goose. Participants don an impressive outfit, complete with a parachute, and launch their bodies off a cliff hoping to "fly" for miles before landing.

We can do anything, right? Fly? Why not? Let's push every limit, even ones that deny basic biology. Pushing our limits is not inherently bad. Olympic gymnasts remind me of the nimble, agile brilliance that is the human body. Yet eventually we must realize we cannot do life in a wingsuit. We are limited. We do not have ever-expanding capacities. Revealing our true selves means accepting limits.

Cultural applause goes to the woman who gets it all done: killer career, top-notch family, nonprofit board, and of course stunning looks. If you wrinkle this page with, "No, I can't do it," don't expect support. People will lament, "What do you mean, you can't? You did it last year." It is easier to say yes to one more thing, do a halfway job, then spin it to sound like it was great or cover it over in a pile of excuses.

Setting limits brings loss, and loss means grief. Who has time to grieve? You already feel bad about all you are missing out on, so why make a point of dwelling there? Absurd. But honestly, God created limits so that we might live well. We are not meant to skim along the surface, bouncing in and out of limitless moments. We are meant to dive deep into life—to soak up the last rays of summer and catch the first hint of autumn air, to look into the eyes of our friend or child and see the face of God. Life is for us to sense, feel, become awash in. The irony is that without limits, our greatest fears come true. We will miss out!

Leaning into limits leads us away from fragmentation. It is movement toward wholeness and the true you, a nod toward healing and soul restoration. The things of the soul move slowly, emerging and evolving over time. Embracing limits dismantles the grandiosity of busyness and being constantly on the go. It unmasks the bloated self we try to earn through posting, "Look where I've been. Look who I know. Look what I've done." Limits give space for our real life stories to emerge. When the ego inflation that comes through busyness is put on hold, the beauty and vulnerability of being human surfaces.

Limits keep us in the present. Limits allow relationships to flourish. Limits make space for our calling to become clear. Your calling is your purpose, the place you move and serve best in this world. Calling is demonstrated as we make choices about what is life giving or life thwarting to us. If we slam down a cup of coffee and holler yes to everything, we may never recognize what brings us joy or sadness. God's beautiful, true you will emerge most clearly within a life of limits. Consider how Mary limited her future options by saying yes to God and the incredible limits of an unplanned pregnancy. "I am the Lord's servant. May your word to me be fulfilled" (Luke 1:38). Within these limits, God made her part of a story that saved us all.

Mary didn't need to go everywhere and meet everyone to have a story that mattered. She needed to be present to the miracle that was taking place in her life in the hard drama of every day. Even Paul, whose industry established many churches, knew his limits. He wrote, "We, however, will not boast beyond proper limits, but will confine our boasting to the sphere of service God himself has assigned to us. . . . Neither do we go beyond our limits" (2 Corinthians 10:13-15). Paul, Jesus, Mary and you—all of us have human limitations. God's beautiful purpose is realized within these limits. In fact, our limits give God room to work.

FLOURISHING

None of us set out to be shallow and half attentive, but it happens when we are zoned out and beyond our limits. I (Tracey) stand in front of our elementary school waiting for my children and watching all of the parents (myself included) trolling through our phones to pick up the one more email that needs attention. We stand there, a mob of several hundred parents, together yet alone. Then we head home and wonder why there is loneliness and ache in the soul. Why does it feel like we've not connected with anyone all day?

It feels this way because we did not recognize our limits and stay present to the moment. Studies on multitasking seem to indicate that our two-lobed brain wasn't designed to do multiple tasks simultaneously. In 2005, Glenn Wilson of King's College London University monitored the IQ of employees throughout the day. He found the average worker's functioning IQ dropped ten points when multitasking, the equivalent of a full night's sleep. We can do multiple tasks sequentially and even quickly, but every time we shift attention we lose presence, productivity and even happiness.[2] We move from fullness to fragments.

If we want more happiness, more love, more of God in our lives, multitasking will not land us there. We must embrace our actual life rather than the one that somehow seems better from afar. Anna Quindlen wrote, "The thing that is really hard and really amazing is giving up on being perfect and beginning the work of becoming yourself." To become ourselves we must slow down, embrace some limits, grieve some losses and be present to what is. *If* we embrace our limits, *then* life will begin to feel more whole and honest, and we can be the sort of women who help others put some of their fragmented pieces back together.

JOURNAL AND PRACTICE

1. Make a list of what distracts you from giving your full presence to each of the following:

   - work

   - friends

   - serving

   - family

   - spouse

   - church

2. Choose one of these places and practice being fully present to it this week.

3. Practice fifteen minutes of presence. Pick a person from your life and sit knee to knee, eyeball to eyeball with them for a full fifteen minutes (yes, this can feel super awkward!). No phone. No laptop. No distractions. Give them your full and undivided attention. Ask them to tell you about their day or anything they might be currently thinking. How does listening and looking at someone for fifteen minutes make you feel?

4. Trusted friends and family may have a different sense of our limits than we do. Ask them where they see fragmentation in your life and where you might need limits. Share your own perspective with them as well.

5. Practice no spontaneous "yeses" for a month. When someone asks you to do something say, "I'll get back to you on that," or

"I'll call you back in sixty seconds." Ask yourself, "Do I really want to do this?" When you say no, be intentional about how you fill that slot of time.

6. Catalog the half-finished things in your life. Which of these things are necessary to complete now? Which can wait? Cross off with a dark line the things that can wait in order to give yourself permission to let go of finishing everything now.

7. When we set limits we often let people down. Write a prayer asking God to help them find another person or way to meet their need.

8. Make a list of the things you say yes and no to. Jot the "yeses" in one column and the "noes" in another. After a few weeks of cataloging, look at your list.

   • What do you learn about yourself from this list?

   • What "noes" will eventually become "yeses" in another season?

   • What "yeses" line up with a calling or sweet spot?

   • Notice how you are no better for your "yeses" and no worse for your "noes."

9. Thank God for the opportunities that have been given to you. Ask for wisdom to choose rhythms that give you life.

6

INNER TRUTH

Who, me? You are kidding, right?

ADELE CALHOUN AND
TRACEY BIANCHI

Few of us remember learning to talk, but when you were a toddler, each new word you stammered was a welcomed marvel for siblings, parents, teachers or friends who were riveted by your every utterance. Speech, even our earliest "dada" and "baba," opens doors to intimacy and understanding. It's been said the "golden years" of parenting are those young elementary-school years when children are old enough to chat up their lives with adults and parents before adolescent eye rolls become the norm.

As we grow up we inevitably discover that our words aren't always welcome. Loud siblings fill all the airspace, leaving no room for any other voice. Perhaps a careless teacher, colleague, parent, spouse, pastor or supervisor squashed tender, young ideas with a careless hiss:

- "Your ideas are useless."

- "Who asked you anyway?"

- "You don't honestly think anyone will believe that!"
- "Shh! Not now!"

The condemning look or finger to the lips may have quite literally "shut up" our childhood or adulthood. Learning to fight for your voice and the ability to share your experiences is essential to keeping the true you thriving and influencing the world in a healthy way.

We know that when authority figures inappropriately silence a child's voice self-doubt rolls in like smog, choking off the life of future words. It also teaches children not to trust themselves, their giftedness or their stories. We carry this into adulthood, where cultural, educational, political and religious systems, as well as prejudices and the penchant for stereotypes, repeat the mantras we hear as children. Validation to speak or listen depends on whether or not you have the "right" race, marital status, class, income, theology or gender. Part of the very luxury we have in writing or reading this book is because we live in a culture that allows women to speak in this way and to learn. There are places in this world where women cannot even pick up a simple resource like this book.

When, because of these pressures, we abdicate the voice God has given us, we are not able to bring our truest selves to our part of this world. Without voice we miss the chance to bring forth our truest learnings, longings and wisdom. Yet daring to speak from the true you requires discernment and courage. If we haphazardly spout our opinions or intentionally take aim to hurt with our words, we risk becoming as careless as those who may have harmed us. We must first

- own our motives for speaking
- understand the risks
- sense where we serve God by keeping quiet
- trust where we serve God by speaking up
- discover why there are places we are simply too afraid to say anything

- graciously accept the opportunity to be fully heard
- understand the consequences for the "audience" (whether one or one thousand)

If I take my mouthy American self and suggest to a woman from a different culture that she simply speak up and own her story in a brash, emboldened way, it could mean her very life. If I suggest to my best friend that she step up and demand that promotion, it could risk her job. Using our voice only matters if we understand the listeners and why we feel called to speak in the first place.

GOD GIVES VOICE

Jesus validates voices not on the basis of race, gender, marital status or education but because of fruitfulness and commitment to his purposes. Because Jesus is "the image of the invisible God, the firstborn over all creation" (Colossians 1:15), he is the filter by which we understand who gets to speak and who does not.

God invites us—urges us—to use our voices to help our true you and the true you of others be known. Sure, some of us are teachers, preachers, writers or bloggers, and we work in professions that trade on words. But all of us, regardless of profession or platform, have an invitation from God to speak to the people and situations of our lives. This invitation isn't about airing our negativity and slandering our adversaries. We are invited to contribute to conversations of life, faith, justice and love.

At a time when a woman's testimony had zero credibility—"What could she possibly know?"—Jesus chose disregarded, undervalued women to tell his disciples the good news of his resurrection (Matthew 28:10). In a culture that segregated men and women, Jesus bridged the divide, enjoying conversations and friendships with women. He was progressive and intentional in his repartee with women. His comfort level with them was so unusual that men were often incensed or surprised (see the story of the woman at the well in John 4, for example). Jesus had the grace to hear women out (Mark 5:25-34; 7:25-30), which is jarring when compared to the way the church has historically treated women.

Jesus validated women's voices and treated them with respect (Luke 7:44; 10:38-42). Do we actually believe that Jesus' model of relating to women was paradigmatic? Do we trust that Jesus is the lens through which we read Paul's letters to particular first-century churches? Will we interpret the written word through the Living Word? If our answer is yes, this is the platform from which we can speak.

Jesus' disciples had a hard time believing his treatment of women was ever to be their norm. They were territorial about who could and could not speak, including men. When John sees someone driving out demons in Jesus name, he hollers, "Teacher . . . we told him to stop, because he was not one of us." But Jesus said, "Do not stop him. For no one who does a miracle in my name can in the next moment say anything bad about me, for whoever is not against us is for us. Truly I tell you, anyone who gives you a cup of water in my name because you belong to the Messiah will certainly not lose their reward" (Mark 9:38-41). Jesus sanctions voices that honor him and his purposes in this world, and that includes you and me.

Many women who attend seminaries will tell you they experience suspicion over their motives for being there. This is one easy example of the contradiction between how the Christian culture often views women versus Jesus' actual views on women. There is a false narrative that says men are in seminary to answer God's call and female students have misunderstood their place or are there to grind an axe.

People use their voices for many reasons: to feel powerful, absorb attention, shape an identity, prove a point, gain a following and on and on. But people can also use their voices to obey, serve, encourage and build the kingdom of God. God alone knows our truest motives. Refuse to let the judgment of others choke off your voice. Jesus gave the benefit of the doubt to people working in his name.

TO SPEAK OR NOT TO SPEAK?

A cost-benefit analysis is essential to running a successful company. When faced with a new project it asks, does the cost outweigh the benefit? If the answer is yes, it's on to the next idea. The art of discernment also includes a cost-benefit analysis. Will what I say lead to greater clarity and love or create hurt and division? Does what I say reflect the generous heart of God or my need to be right?

In life there are times when you sit on your words and trust God's timing. If your boss or colleague is a stressed-out wreck you know it's not the day to add a volatile subject to the agenda. Couples and married folks often tiptoe around their significant other for good reason. It's not wise to brandish the sword every day. Saying less or nothing is often so much more. If you've ever received hate mail or a vicious comment you know that striking back seldom moves the conversation forward and, in fact, pumps the venom.

In Mark 14, Jesus is ambushed with accusations that would cost him his life. He doesn't respond. So the high priest prods him, "'Are you not going to answer? What is this testimony that these men are bringing against you?' But Jesus remained silent and gave no answer." Jesus offers no defense, answers no charges, makes no effort to point out the contradictoriness of the accusations. He doesn't seize the offensive or do something to impede his fate. He's not desperate, resigned or insolent. Jesus doesn't act doomed or like a person on trial for his life. He is calm, knowing, watchful. He is present, alert and awaiting God's plan as redemption inches forward step by unfair step.

When he finally speaks there is no hint that he has been battered by it. He remains stalwart in his person and purposes. When he speaks it is not because he's been triggered. It's because he knows what it is he needs to say. At times, the best way to be heard is to follow Jesus' example and say nothing at all.

SPEAKING UP

Using our voices doesn't guarantee a hearing or receptive listeners. At a former church, preachers stood at the back of the sanctuary and shook hands with the congregation after the service. Each time I (Adele) preached an elderly man would stand in line until he could speak to me. He would grasp my hand, beam at me and say, "Great job. I was surprised at how the sermon spoke to me." He also confessed that he was not convinced women should preach, but he had ears to hear and wouldn't deny when God was speaking to him.

In contrast, Adele shared with me how a major Christian university invited her to speak at three chapel services. They were posted on YouTube and as the "likes" began to tally up the first comment was a slam about losing respect for said university because they let a woman preach. Never mind how true she was to the Word of God; she was a girl. It is fascinating that some of the biggest names in Christian culture are female—women who teach thousands upon thousands each year. They exegete the word of God, and by any measure their delivery style is preaching. Yet many refuse to call themselves preachers because "women don't do that."

These realities lead us to doubting the true self, self-loathing or frustration. *What could I possibly say? I am ridiculous, stupid and my ideas suck. Why does it even matter; if it is true, who cares if a woman or man says it?*

Women as well as men are called to embrace the risky gauntlet of using their voices for the kingdom.

ZELOPHEHAD'S DAUGHTERS

Zelophehad's daughters were concerned about women's rights—specifically, the God-given right to inherit (Numbers 27). They "came forward and stood before Moses, Eleazar the priest, the leaders and the whole assembly" (Numbers 27:1-2), a risky endeavor in an era without much in the way of rights for women. They used their voices to right a wrong, and God commends them for it (Numbers 27:5-8).

It is profoundly humbling to hear the voices of women and girls who have been beaten, trafficked, abused, neglected and silenced. They are daughters of Zelophehad, and they are using their voices to right wrongs. Extrovert or introvert, old or young, we each have a voice that needs to be heard. We need no title, education or platform to back up every thought. If we are women of peace and justice, we have wisdom to share with someone.

We may not identify with super-heroic defenders of justice and peace. Most of us feel utterly average, but we live in an era with more options to use our voices than ever before. Consider the phenomenon of blogging and the way it provides platform and voice for stories. The film *Julie & Julia* is one example. It is estimated that 3.9 million moms in the United States alone are using their voices as bloggers. It's an electronic pandemic of sorts, where other women warm to those who whip up five-hundred-word posts on their foibles and failures. Their mantra is some version of, "I'm a mess. You're a mess. Let's all be messy together." Readers enjoy the solace of knowing that wisdom and hope comes from imperfect and unmanicured lives. Voices like Jen Hatmaker go viral overnight because of their relatability. Suddenly, 3.9 million bits of *true you* trickle out.

RECEIVE YOUR VOICE

I have a friend with a beautiful voice who is afraid to put her stories out there because she compares them to others. "I don't write like Sue Monk Kidd or Anne Lamott, so why bother?" She is paralyzed by self-doubt and fear. Many of us are. We choose a seat in the back row to avoid being vulnerable. We ingest the lie that we have nothing to say and wonder why we feel distant and disengaged, numb. Vulnerability—sharing your story—leads to joy, love and relationship. Vulnerability isn't bad, and it isn't weakness. It is a part of being human and using your voice. It is the way to reclaim all those shushed voices God meant for us to use. Even botched-up, jumbled-up words convey our soul. Words don't have to be perfect, they just have to be shared.

JOURNAL AND PRACTICE

1. Notice how you use your voice for one week. Where do you speak your mind? Where are you quiet? or shushed? or ignored?

Table 1. Using Your Voice

	Monday	Tuesday	Wednesday	Thursday	Friday	Saturday
Work						
Home						
School						
Spouse						
Family						
I refuse to say what I think						
I speak truth with love						

2. What do you learn about your voice?

3. Make a lifeline of the things you have been passionate about. What were you passionate about as a child? teenager? now? Which passions have stuck? What new ones have developed? What is one thing people may not know you are passionate about? This week decide to tell someone about a passion and why it matters to you. Use your voice.

4. Prayer is a way we voice our true you. Sybil MacBeth suggests *Praying in Color.* Check it out. Take a stab at it. Find some markers and doodle on a page the names or events for which you are concerned. Draw around these names using colors, lines, shapes and symbols to express your desires to God. God understands even doodles. Let them help you name your desire and give it to God.

5. As a child what messages did you receive about using your voice?

6. What three things (topics, experiences, etc.) are easy for you to talk about? With whom?

7. What three things are hard for you to talk about?

8. What makes you nervous about using your voice?

9. What parts of your story do you censor?

10. If it is hard to find words for a part of your story, draw or collage it. Use colors to express emotions and images to capture what is hard to say.

7

HOW TO GIVE— AND RECEIVE—YOURSELF

Release your grip. God has more.

ADELE CALHOUN AND
TRACEY BIANCHI

The day after Thanksgiving makes me queasy. After twenty-four hours of rest and praise for the bounty we have, we race out at 3:00 a.m. to shop like mad, in search of more. Black Friday makes my heart feel a little black, and the mindset behind endless accumulation creates a vacuum in the soul. No wonder Vancouver-based artist Ted Dave launched an international protest to Black Friday. He called it "Buy Nothing Day,"[1] one day a year dedicated to *not* consuming and accumulating. It focuses on finding peace and security beyond stuff. But it's been hard to gain traction to publicize this little-known day. Major media networks aren't eager to sell airtime that keeps our wallets at home. Advertisers want us to equate the good life with having more: that Kate Spade handbag will totally change your life, so hop to it and find a good deal. The one who dies with the most toys wins!

Drink the Kool-aid on this one and it will be hard to swallow Jesus' words about how subtracting gives us life: "Whoever wants to be my disciple must deny themselves and take up their cross and follow me. For whoever wants to save their life will lose it, but whoever loses their life for me and for the gospel will save it. What good is it for someone to gain the whole world, yet forfeit their soul?" (Mark 8:34-36). Gaining the world is big business. So, does losing our lives mean resisting the urge to accumulate? Does it mean ditching our goals and dreams, period? How do we think through what we lay down and what we step fully into? It's a delicate maneuver to understand which parts of our lives we should release and, on the flipside, where we sometimes recklessly abdicate power that God meant for us to keep and use. The true you lies somewhere in this mix.

Jesus' words smack our accumulating, acquiring culture in the face. How many of us really believe that self-denial is the way to life? It's like trying to popularize a "buy nothing day." *Who* is the target audience that finds

"losing,"

letting go

and subtracting

more valuable than

winning,

holding on to

and adding?

Jesus lived life to the full. Jesus gives life to the full (John 10:10). Yet Jesus knew that part of his path to life included rejection and a painful death. He told his disciples that following him meant they would also gain life through self-denial and "losing their life." The disciples hate what Jesus is saying. Peter pushes back hard. Thinking he is backing God's plan, he rebukes Jesus' lack of vision and ambition, "Never! . . . This shall never happen to you!" (Matthew 16:22). To Peter, it was the time for Jesus to reach out for more, not risk losing his life. Power up.

Carpe diem! Peter's religious fervor and concern for Jesus are real, but his ego is tangled up with getting perks, having power and accumulating the success that come with being part of Jesus' entourage. Peter wants Jesus to play his power right, so that he accumulates more status, power and authority. Any version of a future that includes rejection, suffering, losing and letting go is not on Peter's agenda—even if it is God's agenda.

Jesus recognizes the tantalizing deception in Peter's plan and responds fiercely, "Get behind me, Satan! You are a stumbling block to me; you do not have in mind the concerns of God, but merely human concerns" (Matthew 16:23). Jesus knows he can "stumble" over his ego too. Calling all the shots, choosing success, following his own agenda—it held human appeal for him. Playing it safe and padding your life with comforts, controls and shortcuts to success sounds good, and Satan had already tempted Jesus with the notion that suffering and death were the worst things that could happen to him (Matthew 4). Peter unwittingly swallowed the deception. He was totally convinced that suffering was the worst thing that could happen to Jesus.

Much to Peter's chagrin, Jesus lets go and upholds that God can actually win through losing. Jesus trusts that suffering doesn't have to be the worst thing that happens to him (or us). He risks that self-denial might actually yield fruit, like life, newness and growth.

INTERNALIZED MESSAGES

In a world of unknown futures it is hard to sell the goodness of letting go and self-denial over buying, having and powering up. Most of us have limited resources. If we don't look after ourselves, who will? It just makes sense to accumulate, amass and pad our lives against privation. To focus on our own well-being and the well-being of those we love seems prudent, not selfish. Is Jesus really asking us to

- let go of our resources?
- downsize our wants, preferences and opportunities?
- subtract from our small pot?
- put others' needs ahead of our own and those of our people?

And is there more to it? Is Jesus actually asking us to let go of who we are? What happens to the true you when we give so much away?

As women it is so easy to give up the wrong things. Religion, family and culture all weigh in with expectations about what women should "lay down for God and country." Early on girls begin internalizing self-sacrificing messages. We are often taught and nurtured to become "mommy's little helpers." Girls let go of who they are and what they want so someone else can be happy, fed, educated or free to go play outside. When self-denying behavior is praised and self-asserting behavior judged or punished, it is hardly any wonder that swaths of girls and women give up their own needs, voices and wants to serve. And when religion and culture unilaterally reinforce this message, it can be hard not to internalize a doormat identity. So how exactly are women to respond to Jesus' call to lose our lives to find them?

Often churches press the biblical injunction for service on women more than men, yet shockingly, in the gospels Jesus seems to focus this message on men. Of course, Jesus' call to deny ourselves is for everyone, but it can be skewed to mean that what women think and want matters less than what brothers, male colleagues, husbands, church authorities and male leaders think and want. When women misinterpret Jesus' words as a diminishing message they can overlook the goodness of their created being and give away responsibility for their own unique gifting and talents. In its most extreme form, the message of laying down one's life can put women in positions where they are used and abused.

Clearly many men don't have to be in charge, take control or be at the top of some hierarchy. They want to share the responsibility and journey with women. We both have colleagues, husbands and male friends who want to share responsibility for work, family and faith evenly. They want Jesus' message of laying down one's life to be an equal-opportunity clause.

So what does Jesus mean when he says, "Deny yourself and take up your cross"? Are women to take no thought of their gifts, potential and calling? Is it all subsumed in what others need and want? We believe the only way to answer this question is to watch how Jesus treats women in a historical context where women's thoughts, talents and dreams were irrelevant.

JESUS' INVITATIONS TO WOMEN

In Mark 5:21-43, Jesus is en route to heal a male leader's daughter whose life is all but over. He rushes through a crowd and a woman grabs for the hem of his cloak as he races past. Suddenly Jesus feels "power" go out of him. To the annoyance of his disciples, Jesus stops and asks, "Who touched my clothes?" She was a desperate woman who had suffered twelve years of bleeding. At this point any rabbi worth his salt would step away and remind her that a) she shouldn't be out in public, b) she mustn't touch men, and c) he's in a hurry about a matter of life and death. But Jesus is so off the cultural script. He doesn't say anything like this. He doesn't tell her to wait until he has time or that her problem is a "woman's issue" best not discussed in public. Instead Jesus validates the woman and her actions. In the process, the male leader has to lay down his agenda and wait for Jesus and for her. It would have been astounding to anyone in Jesus' day. But Jesus respects what looks likes an inappropriate act and a vaguely superstitious faith. Showing uncustomary honor for her needs, her station and her desire for healing, he says, "Daughter, your faith has healed you. Go in peace and be freed from your suffering."

In Mark 7:24-30, Jesus has a remarkable discussion with an outcast, an insistent Gentile woman who wants Jesus to heal her daughter. The disciples are all about sending her away, but Jesus lingers on and responds with a parable. The woman understands the parable and answers in kind. By doing so she is the first person in the gospels to actually "get" a parable. Jesus is so impressed he says, "For such a reply, you may go; the demon has left your daughter." Once again Jesus listens. He honors a woman's desires and treats her with dignity and kindness.

In Mark 12:41-44, Jesus gathers his disciples and comments to them on the offering of an impoverished woman of no account. He wants them to notice that "this poor widow has put more into the treasury than all the others. They all gave out of their wealth; but she, out of her poverty, put in everything—all she had." Jesus isn't impressed with the biblical equivalent of Donald Trump. He is moved by the generosity of a woman who is virtually invisible to men in his culture. He makes sure others see her as somebody of dignity and worth.

Matthew, Mark and Luke all record an incident in which a scandal-clad woman crashes a party where Jesus is supposed to be the guest of honor. Sobbing, she washes his feet with perfume and dries them with her hair. Simon, the host, and his other male guests are indignant. They only see a scurrilous woman, the town whore, when the reality is that she is trying to offer Jesus a simple courtesy. She wants to wash the feet of Jesus, a hospitality ritual that the host had "overlooked" to embarrass Jesus. The men see only her shameful past, so Jesus asks if they really "see this woman" (Luke 7:36-50). Jesus sees love where others see shame. He sees a broken and contrite heart where others see a stereotype. He sees value where they see trash. He commends her action where others try to tangle up goodness. He gives dignity, saying, "Your sins are forgiven. . . . Your faith has saved you; go in peace."

Of course, what would a book for women be without mentioning the story of Mary and Martha? Mary isn't in the kitchen doing the traditional female thing. She is doing what male rabbinic disciples do. She is exercising her mind, sitting with the men while they learn with their teacher. Martha seems both embarrassed by and annoyed with

Mary. She is vexed at Jesus for not shooing her sister out to prepare food. It is a landmark moment. Will Jesus underscore a woman's secondary role or commend her ability to think and learn? Now is the time for Jesus to put Mary in her right place. All he needs to do is say, "Be a good girl and go help Martha out. Sorry, only male disciples can hang out and learn from me." Instead Jesus says the unthinkable. He praises Mary for choosing what is better (Luke 10:42).

Another curious encounter between Jesus and women happens at his tomb. The male disciples are panic-stricken and in hiding after Jesus' terrorizing death. But the women who followed Jesus were so unimportant to Roman authorities that they could come and go from the tomb with ease. They are the first to see Jesus after his resurrection. Jesus tells the women, "Do not be afraid. Go and tell my brothers to go to Galilee; there they will see me" (Matthew 28:10). The testimony of a woman meant absolutely nothing at that time. Yet Jesus sends the women to the men. They are responsible to proclaim the good news of his resurrection to the disciples. The word *apostle* means "sent one." Isn't it something that the women are the apostles to the apostles? If then, why not now? Jesus affirms women living out of the true selves he sees in them, not the places culture relegates them to.

Search the Scriptures: the woman at the well (John 4), the crippled woman healed on the Sabbath (Luke 13), the parable of the persistent widow (Luke 18). Jesus' interaction with women is culturally and historically different than the norm. He doesn't condemn or diminish or ignore them. Jesus calls women to step into their belovedness, their giftings and full participation in the kingdom—participation that means serving others from this place rather than assumed, second-class servitude.

All Jesus' encounters endorse the status, dignity and value of women as equal to that of men. For centuries on either side of 30 A.D., there is no one with a message more freeing or empowering to women than Jesus Christ. The way he actually treats women and outcasts is a necessary lens for understanding all scriptural texts about the role of women. Seeing ourselves the way God sees us is how we discover our "true you."

A CONSISTENT MESSAGE

Jesus' persistent message to women to step up into their belovedness and agency has a different tone than much of what he says specifically to men about their need to come down. It is important to look at this difference to underscore how differently Jesus saw women than many of the debates today would tell us. Jesus originally said these things to a group of men:

- Jesus taught the apostles, saying: "The kings of the Gentiles lord it over them; and those who exercise authority over them call themselves Benefactors. But you are not to be like that. Instead, the greatest among you should be like the youngest, and the one who rules like the one who serves." (Luke 22:25-26)

- "Why are you so afraid? Do you still have no faith?" (Mark 4:40)

- "You hypocrites!" (Luke 13:15)

- "Unless you change and become like little children, you will never enter the kingdom of heaven. Therefore, whoever takes the lowly position of this child is the greatest in the kingdom of heaven." (Matthew 18:3-4)

- "Woe to you, teachers of the law and Pharisees. . . . Woe to you, blind guides!" (Matthew 23:15-16)

- "What were you arguing about on the road?" But they kept quiet because on the way they had argued about who was the greatest. (Mark 9:33-34)

- [The disciples said,] "Lord, do you want us to call fire down from heaven to destroy them?" But Jesus turned and rebuked them. (Luke 9:54-55)

Jesus is vexed when his male disciples power up. He wants them to notice their motives, blindness, competition, control, entitlement and ambition so they can humble themselves and hand over their lives. Yes, women fall prey to all these characteristics as well, yet it is interesting that the conversations Jesus has with women are so dramatically different.

Yes, Jesus consistently calls *all* disciples to a path of letting go and descent. Yes, he demonstrates this path by descending down farther than anyone before or after him has ever descended. Jesus leaves God's side. He lays down his power. He hands over his life. He says, "God, not my agenda—yours." There is an inexorable letting go at the heart of Jesus' message. The only way to have a full life is to lay our selfie-obsessed ego at Jesus' feet. If our decisions are only about accumulating, moving up and having authority, we miss the abundant life Jesus offers.

Death to our ego isn't about being devalued by God or by men. God loves us all radically, unconditionally, vulnerably–and just for our sake. Jesus' call to "lose your life" isn't a message meant to keep women at the bottom of some cultural heap nor is it licence for the voiceless to be used and abused by other people. Instead, it is to sift through what other voices tell me so that I can deny the selfish, me-centric parts of myself in order to submit to God's will and purposes.

MY EGO

Our history, culture and ego always shape how we hear Jesus' words, "Deny yourself." Jesus knows that some women need to lay down their fear and feelings of worthlessness. Some need to lay down their passivity and take responsibility for their gifts. Only when they do this can they step into their God-given dignity and use their voice. For some of us, to submit to God is to step up and own our belovedness. Jesus knows that other women may need to be reminded to lay down their entitlement and serve someone or something other than their own best interests.

If your identity is tied to being unimportant, pray for courage to take responsibility for the story you have been given. If your identity is tied to being needed, lay down the need to be everyone's everything. If you habitually keep quiet because you don't want to be criticized, lay down your self-doubt and step into your voice. If you habitually dominate the conversation, you may need to look for opportunities to be quiet and listen.

Laying down our lives is always personal and specific. It addresses our egos so that our true selves emerge. When I realize I would rather hurt someone else than suffer a little myself, I have something to lay down. When I notice I'd rather ignore being wronged than address it in a painful conversation, I have something to lay down.

WHAT ABOUT SUBMISSION?

We can both imagine a thousand voices saying, "Yes, but what about Paul's letters referencing silence, submission of wives and the created order?" This small book can't address all the exegetical issues. In short, the texts in question should be read through the context in which Paul wrote them, and in light of what Jesus actually said and how he treated women. Ephesians 5:21-33 frames behavior based on mutual submission between husband and wife. It reads, "Submit to one another out of reverence for Christ. Wives, submit yourselves to your own husbands as you do to the Lord. . . . Husbands, love your wives, just as Christ loved the church and gave himself up for her."

This is not encouragement for husbands to dominate their wives or for wives to accept abusive treatment from their husbands. It does not mean that what he says goes or that the man gets the final say while the woman's voice eventually goes mute, or that he follows his dreams while she ignores hers. Abuse happens when definitions of authority and submission become horribly warped. When husbands control rather than love their wives, the couple needs help. She may need to get out and into a safe place. It is a troubling fact that domestic violence toward women "is just as common within the evangelical churches as anywhere else."[2] There are safe places to go for this help (we list a few in the recommended resources at the end of this book). When women have suffered abuse it is inappropriate to say, "You become your best and most beautiful self by laying down your life."

Women who have become mothers (and we know not all have) understand denying themselves in a unique and decisive way. Children come to a mother and that mom "dies" to peace, quiet, sleep, evenings out, a clean space and time alone. When children grow up and make harmful choices and hate and holler, moms argue and ache but fiercely love. They pace, and pray, and advise, and pay therapists and rehab facilities. Parenting forces vulnerability to worry, fear and anxiety—which is to say suffering. Still, parents pray, spend, yearn, arrange, hope and hold, because dying to their agenda is what it means to love children in ways that make them thrive—ways that help their true selves emerge too.

HAPPINESS IS NOT PAINLESS

There is no fast pass around pain into happiness. Happiness is not hinged to easy relationships; it comes as a result of putting someone else at the center of our lives—through spending our lives rather than hoarding them. It comes through losing our lives and becoming free enough to find them in the process.

Can you recognize the sort of laying down that brings life? For example, if a colleague betrays you, can you release desires to: ruin her? get even? make her suffer? Instead, suffer a little death to the mean-girl thing that came to mind, and lean into the power forgiveness has to set us free. We can refuse to be ruled by the past and its pain.

Barbara Brown Taylor writes,

> You can try to save your own life. You can try to stockpile it, being very, very careful about what you say yes to; being very,

very cautious about whom you let into your life, frisking everyone at the door and letting only the most harmless people inside; and being very, very wary about going outside yourself, venturing forth only under very heavy guard and ready to retreat at the first sign of trouble.[3]

If you decide to safeguard your life—don't expect it to be thrilling. Thrills come when we take a risk. Taylor continues, "The deep secret of Jesus' . . . way to have an abundant life is not to save it but to spend it, to give it away, because life cannot be shut up and saved any more than a bird can be put in a shoebox and stored on a closet shelf."[4] We each have to take up our cross and give our life away. We can walk through suffering and rejection with the love of God in our hearts or run away. Escaping is not a way to life.

MORE FOR THOSE WHO GIVE

Jesus says to stop running from your cross. Stoop down and pick it up. He held in his wounded body the suffering and sin of the world. He held it and refused to transmit it or send it back on the heads of those of us who deserve it. Jesus' refusal to run away from pain not only reconciles us to God but reveals a new way to live—a way in which pain can be suffered, born and transformed, not transmitted. Place your unresolved pain, fear and suffering into Jesus' wounds and take up your cross.

In the end the only people really free are those who know their lives are not their own—who celebrate the "true you" that is meant to have voice and dance and create and bring beauty to this world while laying down the selfish, conceited desires to dominate and own. Free people can take risks with who they are and what they have rather than squirrel it away for their own use. They can be vulnerable, which means they will hurt, suffer, forgive and die—redemptively, creatively—knowing that there is always more life for those who give themselves to Jesus.

JOURNAL AND PRACTICE

1. Make a collage (with magazines or as a board on Pinterest) of the joy, hope and creativity you would like to find in your life. Clip photos and pictures that get at your deepest desires and longings. What is God inviting you to explore? Where would you go? Whom might you befriend? What could you study? What new thing might you try?

2. Make a "let go and let God" box. You can choose a box or make and decorate your own. When you come to something you feel God is asking you to let go of, write it down on a piece of paper and put it in the box. Offer this part of your life to God. Pray a prayer of quiet trust acknowledging how you are willing to lose your life to find it. After several months look back at what is in the box. Can you see how letting go is freeing you up to receive life?

3. What is something you are hanging on to, something you don't want to lose or give away? This week decide how you can give this particular thing, or something that represents it, away. For instance, if someone admires one of your possessions (vase, cell-phone case, earrings, etc.), give it away. Find out how free you are to lose something in order to find life.

4. Practice the Prayer of Examen. At the end of each day ask yourself one of these questions:

   - What gave me life today? What drained life away?

   - What was my high? My low?

   - Where did I encounter love, joy and peace? Where did fear, meanness and criticism surface?

5. Let your answer shape a prayer to God.

6. Losing our lives means a little suffering—but it also means

freedom from a demanding ego. Check out how free you are by logging your responses to the following questions:

- Can you let go of the notion that you are a miserable failure?

- Can you receive a moment the way it arrives? Or do you have to try to force it into being what you want?

- Does your importance depend on your colleagues', children's, friends' or spouse's actions and accomplishments? Can you speak of them without bragging—or apologizing?

- What happens to you when others don't need your help?

- Can you listen to and receive what a friend or an adversary says about you and not defend or attack?

- Do you believe others, even "enemies," are valuable to you because they see you in a way you don't see yourself?

- Can you let go of the belief that competition, image and having more defines you?

- When people don't agree with you, can you listen to them rather than judge them?

7. Look back at your responses. Is there a pattern that forms? Where is God inviting you to lose your life so you can find it?

8. Becoming disenchanted with our egos is always a journey. Where are you trying to elbow your way into someone else's center? What are you wanting to get or hang on to? Is God inviting you to let go of your ego a bit so that another might find life and encouragement, or even gain their spotlight moment?

9. What calling (chance to use your gifts or passions) keeps coming to your mind? When did it begin? How do you need to use your voice to realize this call? What do you need to let go of to live into this call? Visualize this by writing it out in four columns, one for each of these words: "call," "when," "voice" and "let go."

8

24/6 LIVING

Back porch swing. Napping with God.

LESA ENGTHALLER

Most mornings begin for me (Tracey) in the same jarring fashion. I "snooze" my way past any chance of uninterrupted coffee or alone time before my three young children bombard me with a litany of needs. Fixing breakfast, I scroll through my phone as messages ping and taunt me. I'm already behind. The babysitter is stuck in traffic. Urgent meetings loom. Relentless youth sports encroach. And apparently it is my turn to provide snacks after baseball. I hate when it's my turn for snacks. Each day is a flurry of backpacks, getting to school, getting to work, arguing, band practice, homework, dinner and the gnawing reminder that I'm near middle age and should probably exercise or something. Can I down two Red Bulls with breakfast?

I'm aware that Sabbath practices exist, that I was not made for 24/7 adrenaline, and that God built into our lives the need for rest and renewal. I catch a whiff of this on occasion. My soul knows it is true, yet it feels overwhelming to think of slowing down and considering what Sabbath keeping might mean for my life. Shiny objects abound. As my friend says, "The new holier than thou is busier than thou."

Sometimes I (Adele) work flat out for ten or twelve days in a row. I don't intend to do this. People get sick, appointments get moved, guests come to stay, a book or sermon needs writing, the garden wants tending, a friend needs a meal, and I think that resting won't get these things done. I tell myself, "Things will slow down in a week or so." At times my nonstop availability seems necessary. Yet I know it is dangerous. My flat-out living bleeds into all my relationships, subtly conveying messages:

- Busy equals important

- You must flex for me.

- My schedule takes priority

- If you aren't flat out your life is worth less than those who live relentlessly.

According to Harvard economics professor Juliet Schor, professional women report that their "leisure time has declined by as much as one third since the early 1970s."[1] People don't rest more; they rest less. Shore contends that the past forty years have in fact delivered less leisure time and more stress. In her book *The Overworked American*, Schor points out that, in most of the developing world, with industrial and technological advances came an increase in leisure. It took less time to manufacture an item or complete a task which resulted in more leisure time. However, in the United States, we balked at an increase in leisure and opted instead to produce more. The result? An overworked, overstimulated, overconsuming, overaddicted culture in which stress-related diseases and sleep disorders have exploded. We live beyond our limits hoping to achieve beyond our limits.

SUPER HEROICS

The apostle Paul seems to have understood the lure of this when he wrote, "We, however, will not boast beyond proper limits, but will confine our boasting to the sphere of service God himself has assigned to us, a sphere that also includes you. . . . For we do not want to boast about work already done in someone else's territory" (2 Corinthians 10:13-16). If any apostle leaned toward workaholism it was Paul. Before converting to Christianity he was an ardent defender of Jewish orthodoxy. Hunting down and persecuting Christian heretics kept him busy and essential. After his Damascus Road encounter with Jesus, Paul's passion for truth continued to drive him. He wrote more letters than any other New Testament author. He traveled, preached, authored, was imprisoned, shipwrecked and challenged regularly for his faith, yet he persevered. Some might say Paul was an overachiever. But his accolades and accomplishments did not define him. The God he loved and the community that cared for him were what mattered. He found time for Sabbath life.

God crafted a role for Paul to play, but notice what God did not say. God did not demand that Paul himself go to every province in Asia and plant every church. He didn't need to run every errand, train every pastor and encourage everyone. Paul had limits of time, space, energy, vocation and season, as well as a "thorn in his flesh" (2 Corinthians 12). Paul prayed that this physical ailment (we still don't know what it was) would go away. It was a suffering that slowed him down. Yet the thorn remained. Paul's true self was limited to a physical body that needed rest and renewal. Perhaps this thorn curbed Paul's self-importance, reminding him of his limits—limits that made space for rest, silence and time with God.

Americans have a fascination with superheroes. Our icons of film and pop culture include seemingly regular folks who conjure up extraordinary abilities when the need arises. Who among us would not want their powers to rescue, race, fly, climb and intervene on behalf of those in need? On most days I'd take something as small as the ability to dodge rush-hour traffic so that I could do more, faster.

Suppose we took Paul's encouragement from 2 Corinthians 10 and confined our lives to the territory that God has given us by embracing the Sabbath rhythm of 24/6 living? Would we be less or more than who we are? How does perpetual motion injure the true you that was designed for seasons of rest?

24/7 LIFE

Only machines can operate 24/7, and even they need to be turned off on occasion to grease a few brackets or seams. Rest is part of God's creation story. God designed us with brains that dabble in astrophysics and neurosurgery. God gave us bodies that break Olympic records, dance or run marathons. Yet both our brains and our bodies need rest. Sabbath is God's gift, a way of being honest about and honoring depletion. The goodness of Sabbath and the owning of our limits is profound. Sabbath

- reminds us that God is present in all things—all seven days.
- invites us to stop and listen to what our bodies are telling us.
- reminds us that both work and rest bring pleasure.
- dismantles our addiction to self-importance.
- reminds us that community is essential.
- nurtures an appreciation for others.

Still, we are addicted to momentum, and addictions are hard to break. A friend blithely confided, "I don't practice Sabbath. I never have. I never will. I like to be busy 24/7." Slowing down to rest doesn't appeal to everyone. When you were a child, you probably shrieked like a cat to avoid a nap. Most kids do. They desperately fear missing out on something if their eyes close. The same is true for many of us. We may crave a good nap, but feelings of unproductiveness and frustration surface when we lie down and absorb a silent room. Facing who we are when we aren't busy can actually be more difficult than over-working. It's when we stop and sit with the silence, or the people we say we love, that we face our true selves. To be a human *doing* can be easier than a being a human *being*.

We say we want a healthier life, a balance. So we cram yoga and errands into a short lunch hour. Even resting up can become stressful. *What if I run out of time for it?* Sabbath is God's way to break this pattern with the gift of 24/6 living. At first, setting twenty-four hours aside can feel like God has pulled up the emergency brake on a train. The railcar has stopped, but the momentum of life crashes in from behind. *What am I missing out on? I can't possibly live without those twenty-four hours every week!* Yet this might just be the most productive of all our time, as it makes space for intangible and precious things that are hard to quantify: relationships, gratitude, love, God. Those twenty-four hours are about what matters most to us. When we experience that centered place we live differently during the other six days.

24/6

Nancy and Matthew Sleeth practice and write about their sabbath stories together. Matthew, a former ER doctor, explains how neglecting a rest day affects his life and the life of his patients:

> As an A+ personality type, I felt the ramifications in my health, my marriage, and my work. Then a decade ago, my family switched from a 24/7 way of life to a 24/6 rhythm. On multiple levels, taking a weekly "Stop Day" saved our lives. It can save yours, too. Everything has limits, including us. To believe we don't have boundaries is hubris. . . . Perhaps the best thing we can do for the peace and healing of our country is to take a weekly day of rest, beginning now.[2]

Sabbath invites us to say no to work and to own the fact that the complex operations of life will actually find a way to move forward without our involvement. It embraces and respects the true reality of human bodies. Sabbath invites us to do more than just subtract work

from our lives; it invites us to fill that space with people, worship, togetherness and whole living. The idol of exhaustion inevitably en-
croaches on this sacred Sabbath space. We boast of how tired we are
and rationalize that, because it's all good stuff, God understands what
it means for us to keep the world spinning.

For millennia devout Jews have stopped from sundown Friday until
sundown Saturday. On Sabbath they leave producing, achieving and
making a name for oneself to God. They hand the weight of life to
God for twenty-four hours and lean into God's rhythm. Embracing
the goodness of a day without a role or a to-do list reminds them that
they are no longer slaves in Egypt. They have discretion over their time
and can settle into the restful identity that comes with being loved for
being your true you—nothing more and nothing less.

Sabbath is an invitation rather than an instruction. Exodus 20:8-10
reads: "Remember the Sabbath day by keeping it holy. Six days you
shall labor and do all your work, but the seventh day is a sabbath to the
Lord your God." The invitation is for us as God's people to remember
that we are distinctly free. The Israelites had been slaves in Egypt for
four hundred years. Ancient Egypt functioned on a ten-day workweek.
What a relief and gift it was to know that God intended Israel to rest.
If we can't stop working to rest we are just slaves to a paycheck.

SO HOW DO I TAKE A SABBATH?

When I (Adele) was single I found Sabbath my loneliest day. People
went to church and then home to their families, and if I hadn't planned
something I often went back to the poignancy of an empty apartment,
afternoon and evening. Yes, it was a slower time, but I had to embrace
the goodness of 24/6 living even when I felt less connected to friends
or family than I had hoped. I had to learn how to settle into my own
company and my own choices about God's gift day.

When I (Tracey) had a newborn and two toddlers underfoot I
thought Sabbath was a joke. I remember sitting through a sermon on

keeping Sabbath when I had a colicky six-week-old who screamed incessantly. I was sleep deprived and nursing every two to three hours. Sermonizing on rest made me furious. What fool of a pastor would tell young moms to take a Sabbath? But God intends Sabbath for new moms and also for caregivers, rescue workers, friends holding vigil over a hospice bed, people holding down three jobs, in prison or locked up in treacherous situations. Sometimes Sabbath is elusive and doesn't fit into twenty-four tidy hours. Rest and peace come in small spaces. It is not twenty-four hours with your feet up, but perhaps it can be twenty-four hours of intentional time in whatever way makes sense in your situation.

Does Sabbath mean

- sitting at home alone?
- rejecting all games and recreation?
- pulling the plug on all technology?
- avoiding the NFL or the trail and beaches?
- spending all day at church?
- having to cook or getting to cook?

When Doug and Adele take their Friday Sabbath they try to re-source their introverted natures. They sleep in, pay attention to God, get out in nature, walk, kayak, see a movie, have dinner with friends. They breathe in the oxygen and goodness of 24/6. People who practice Sabbath fall in love with the rhythm, and they don't want to go back. Re-entry can feel like the last day of a vacation, we long for it to carry on because honoring ourselves and God gives us life.

A SABBATH EXPERIMENT

Why not try experimenting with Sabbath however it works for your life stage? Sabbath for Adele, whose children are grown, looks dramatically different than for Tracey. What would it look like if we all decided to be intentional, adamant and assertive about Sabbath's 24/6 rhythm? Here's the math:

- One-seventh of every week is rest.

- This means one-seventh of your life is rest.

- That's fifty-two days of rest in one year.

- That adds up to 364 days in seven years, or ten years of Sabbath if you live seventy years!

Remove these days from your life and the lives of others and an ocean of time spent with God and the family of God goes missing. What's missing from our lives does matter. Rest, love and forbearance are not the subjects of news headlines or debates, but they are the things that make society civil and life worth living. They are the things we find when we stop and rest.

STARTING A SABBATH EXPERIMENT

Plan. Make a plan. Set a period of time—ideally twenty-four hours— as an act of trust in God. (If not twenty-four hours then however many hours work for you. Maybe you break it into segments. Sabbath doesn't have to happen all at once on Sunday.) Let's stop trying to hold it all together and instead risk on an unlimited God who is running the world while we rest into our limits. The catch is to plan on taking the time. Like putting in a request for vacation days, you need to block out the space on your calendar and relentlessly protect that time or Sabbath will not happen.

Rest. Be intentional about what needs to be removed from your day so that you can truly rest your body and mind. You may fear that if you don't keep life running and customers satisfied that all will be lost. You will fail. Fear of failure can feel more scary than exhaustion, and it certainly crouches at the door of your rest. Yet it is not taking the rest that can kill you. The Jews prepared for Sabbath so their seventh day did not mean doing all the stuff they didn't get done throughout the week. Sabbath is not the day we clean the closet, mow the lawn, do our taxes and paint the hall. It's not a day for other work. It is a day for rest, so let go of everything that is work for you. Maybe it means not checking email or checking it only once during the day. Maybe it means turning off the phone or avoiding social media.

Delight. Delight in God and one another on the Sabbath. What does a perfect day look like to you? What would delight your heart and feel like a taste of heaven? A meal with family and friends? A nap? Games with people you adore? Making love to your spouse? A book and thirty minutes of quiet? Sabbath is a way to delight in the goodness of being alive. We do what brings us into the fullest presence of God and other people. Take an inventory of what makes you feel light and easy. What brings a smile to your face at the thought of it? Doing that which brings us joy reminds us that God delights in us and designed us to delight in the goodness of life.

Remember you are free. 24/7 living means neglecting our limits, endangering our health and becoming a slave to something. Sabbath gives us a free day. We can negotiate how to spend this day; the details are up to us. Jesus himself said that the Sabbath was made for people and not the other way around. Do not obsess over the details, for this is not freeing; the details can bury and trap us. Hold loosely to the plan for a Sabbath day or the plan itself will enslave you. If you can reconfigure how you think about your time you will find the Sabbath as freeing rather than limiting. If keeping the Sabbath always feels like work then somehow the point has been missed.

Worship together. Sabbath includes both individual and corporate worship. Corporate worship defies the narcissism of 24/7 living. When we gather with people we did not choose, to listen to music and sermons that we may or may not like, we are saying something about who and what matters most. It's not my taste, family and time that matters most, but God—the same God who wants to undo the self-importance at the center of my life. Worship and Sabbath keeping reveal that God matters more than anything else. Being part of a community of faith humbles and grows us into people who can let go of our own way and receive what is given. Many Christians celebrate their Sabbath on Sunday and begin this day with corporate worship with their faith community.

RETURNING TO THE WORLD

We rest so that we can return. One of the reasons God gives us Sabbath is so that we can re-engage with the world, returning with perhaps a renewed vision of what God calls us to or a refreshed body ready for kingdom work. We can return refreshed, re-energized, more gracious and patient, more thankful and nourished, well fed and well loved. We return to the world with grace for the journey.

Go easy on yourself when you experiment with Sabbath. It is not easy, and a drive for perfection defeats the purpose. Give yourself and your friends and family grace. Fortunately Sabbath is about giving you the time you need to figure it out. Learn to rest in God for what is unfinished in you. Don't rush. Go slowly—there is so little time.

JOURNAL AND PRACTICE

1. What would it look like for your family to celebrate and rest on a regular weekly basis? What is doable? What would be fun? What would help you worship God? Ask this of aging parents or young children, neighbors or friends you may Skype with long distance, whomever you love and want to invite into your Sabbath practices.

2. Try a simplify experiment with friends, your small group or family. Each person comes up with a list of ways they can downsize, limit clutter, get rid of stuff, free up time, consume less, etc. For one week they practice their list. What is it like? The one who wins is not the one with the longest list but the best follow-through.

3. Plan your dream Sabbath day. How will you worship? Your day can include church, a walk on the beach, a picnic with friends, a nap, an hour to run by yourself, making cookies and dipping them in milk. Do what gives you life. Enjoy and offer your day to God.

4. What sort of things bring you life? How are you integrating life-giving things into your current season?

5. Write a story about a perfect Sabbath day. What parts of this perfect day could actually happen now in the life you have?

6. What messages do you tell yourself about Sabbath keeping? How do these messages shape your reality?

9

APPROACHING GOD

Talking at God. Being with God.

ADELE CALHOUN AND
TRACEY BIANCHI

What is your prayer story like? Strong? Devoted? Embarrassing? Nonexistent? We have friends that say, "I talk to God all day long," while others wring their hands over their puny, minimalist prayers. Rocket prayers. Panic prayers. Childish prayers.

"OMG. Help me!"

"Jesus, can I trust you?"

"GOD, DO YOU HEAR ME?"

"Please, God, give me, give me, give me! Please!"

We both have days when we wonder if God can be trusted and if ranting counts as prayer. It's then we remind ourselves that we all belong to a global, historic company of women unlike us in many ways but so much like us in that their souls all yearn. These women have wildly personal and unique prayer lives—women like Eve, Hannah, Mary, Teresa of Avila, Barbara Brown Taylor and that sweet, prayerful old lady that lived on your block growing up.

Anne Lamott's suggestion to pray, "Help, thanks, wow,"[1] is simple yet stunning. Sybil MacBeth[2] got Adele praying in color. Tracey would rather pass out than try to pray in color. Thank God someone said, "Pray as you can, not as you can't." Some of us may be quick to dive into the darkest depths of God. But others of us need permission to flap around on the surface with goggles and a snorkel—because that is where we are as of now.

We find what works. We grope around with the complications of our lives. It's okay to be where we are with God. What matters is that we find some way to communicate with the Holy. Only when we pray and know God can our truest selves come out.

Barbara Brown Taylor, an accomplished preacher and theologian, admits to being a rank beginner when it comes to prayer: "I would rather show someone my checkbook stubs than talk about my prayer life. I would rather confess that I am a rotten god-mother, that I struggle with my weight, that I fear I am overly fond of Bombay Sapphire gin martinis than confess that I am a prayer-weakling. To say I love God but I do not pray much is like saying I love life but I do not breathe much."[3]

Of course there are prayer warriors who ruin their knees battling back the forces of darkness with their intercessions. They have visions; they see light. They pray through. I (Adele) am in awe, for I identify more with the prayer-weakling thing. I bought a prie-dieu (a prayer bench for kneeling) hoping the sight of it would draw me to my knees. I look at it way more than I kneel on it. But the sight reminds me to stick with it, to begin to pray again and again and settle into being a lifetime beginner in prayer.

Adele a beginner? I (Tracey) look at Adele and think she is the poster child for prayer. Her first book, *Spiritual Disciplines Handbook*, is filled with ways to boost a prayer life. She lists ideas like prayer journals, prayer walks, prayer books, healing prayer, contemplative prayer, breath prayer, praying the hours, etc.[4] I skim her table of contents and think she knows how to make space in her life for God. And me—I intend to pray, but I fall into bed with half-finished heartaches and prayers racing through my mind. I guess we are both beginners who want to pray. But wanting and intending are just a start. Prayer is part of a relationship, and like any relationship, there are days of sheer joy and flat dissatisfaction.

TRUST ISSUES

Perhaps it is hard to bring our true you to pray because we did not get the life we wanted. God seems to be donning flip-flops in Maui while we are in crisis. As we bounce along in the turbulence of life, we often discover trust issues spilling into our relationship with God. We cannot lay the deepest parts of our souls out if we don't feel safe.

Prayer describes a relationship. God invites you into a circle of belonging, a circle of trust and love, where you are free to give and receive, free to come and go. Growing in a way that brings out the truest you is always a risk. It means keeping your heart open and engaged through seasons of longing and equanimity, closeness and distance, rage and hope. It means being honest about the coldness, emptiness, fervor, longing, lament, anger, gratitude, love, joy and hate that is on the inside.

During some seasons fire falls, and our hearts burn with love for God (Acts 2). Other times we slouch and shuffle along like adolescents barely on speaking terms with their parents. Once in a while we lean in with our personal brand of vitriol and give God an acidic stare. At times, past experiences warn us to beware of trusting anyone with the desires and prayers of our heart.

Perhaps someone who should have been safe abused or abandoned us—maybe that person was an uncle, or brother, or father. This makes us leery to risk on God, "Our Father, who art in heaven . . . " Some among us struggle to trust that any father has our best interests at heart.

If you struggle with trust issues and don't feel safe with God, you travel with good companions. Consider these ragged, raw prayers:

- Psalm 22:1-2: "My God, my God, why have you forsaken me? Why are you so far from saving me, so far from my cries of anguish? My God, I cry out by day, but you do not answer, by night, but I find no rest."

- Psalm 44:23-24: "Awake, Lord! Why do you sleep? Rouse yourself! Do not reject us forever. Why do you hide your face and forget our misery and oppression?"

These prayers risk vulnerability. They voice trust issues. Does God care? Will God abandon, and punish? Is God fickle—coming and going based on what I do? When we believe God is harsh, angry and ready to abandon or punish, we tap into the same ancient vein of Eve's trust issues.

The serpent convinced our sister Eve (and brother Adam) that God could not be trusted. They questioned whether God was really out for their best interests. The Creator must be holding out on them—reserving one special tree—marking it off for God alone. Surely, a loving God would not deprive them. How could God withhold something so obviously valued? Maybe God wasn't as good as they thought.

The dark one wanted Eve to believe this lie, knowing that if we distrust God's goodness it is logical to then suspect God's intentions. If God cannot be trusted then we alone must make our decisions about what is good and bad. Eve was deceived about God, and she broke the circle of love and trust between God and herself. She believed the lie—that God couldn't bear the *real* of their relationship.

MENDING THE CIRCLE OF TRUST AND LOVE

When the circle of love and trust between God and Eve broke down, the once free and easy dialogue with God was fraught with shame and anxiety. What would God say and do? Eve couldn't bear to face her Creator. Normal had changed. That routine walk with God in the cool of the day now felt so chilled and menacing that both Eve and Adam bolted for cover. When God does find them, the first shout holds rationalization, denial, blame and fear. From that moment on mistrust metastasizes into their conversations with God and one another. The never-ending project of sewing fig leaves together to hide the true you is up and running.

Fig leaves of education, success, accomplishment and wealth often hide our fear of being known and seen. God longs to free us from the hiding that warps our relationships. We know this because God responds to Adam and Eve's fears and shame with love. God relates with love, taking the initiative to find, clothe, protect and rescue them (Genesis 3). Eve didn't have to get her mess together before the circle of love and belonging could mend. The Creator reached into the debris with encompassing, unconditional, given, endless, comprehensive and unchanging love. Even when God turned Adam and Eve out of paradise it was to protect them from the temptation to eat from the Tree of Life and end up with an eternity of brokenness. An angel with a flaming sword may not have seemed loving, but that angel was protection and a sign of God's good intentions. God is love, always and forever (1 John 4:8). God's love is never quenched by our imperfect prayers and mess. The Song of Songs says, "Many waters cannot quench love; rivers cannot sweep it away" (Song of Songs 8:7). The Trinity holds everything and everyone in an embrace of self-giving love.

God's intentions toward us are so good that God comes in person, in Jesus, to rescue us. Jesus says plainly that he did not come to condemn and punish but to give life to the full (John 3:17; 10:10). No matter what has happened to you. No matter what you have done. God's love for you remains intact.

You may have been on the paid staff of hell, and all you mutter is "Oh God, I hate me, help me." Yet those words fall onto ears of love. When you are vulnerable enough to risk exposing your true you to God, the circle of love and trust will hold you. This is the root of prayer. "Prayer is taking a chance that against all odds and past history, we are loved and chosen, and do not have to get it together before we show up."[5]

USING OUR VOICES TO PRAY

Say we are working on our trust issues with God. Say we are leaning into that circle of love and trust and trying to bring out our true you. What comes next? After all, Isaiah saw the Lord and cried out, "Woe to me!" (Isaiah 6). Samson's parents saw God and thought they might die (Judges 13:22). The Israelites heard the voice of God and never wanted to hear it again (Exodus 20:19). So how are we to come before a holy, holy, holy God?

The unexplored territory at the edges of ancient maps was often inscribed with three words, "Here be dragons." Uncharted territory was unknown, eerie. Prayer can feel like we've reached the edge of the map. Do we dare to set up camp on the nervous edge of where we end and God begins? What if we walk straight into the mist and never return? Do we talk? Listen? Monologue? Praise? Once we say, "God, it's me," what comes next? Is there a proper posture? Is it "ay-men" or "awe-men"?

I (Tracey) grew up saying a prayer I'm not going to teach my children: "Now I lay me down to sleep, I pray the Lord my soul to keep. And if I die before I wake, I pray the Lord my soul to take." It feels a bit traumatic to me when I reflect back, and yet it was the only prayer I knew for the first twelve years of my life. My grandmother taught it to me, and while it unnerved me, it strangely brought me comfort for it was the only way I knew to talk to God. Adele's first prayers were simple and rote; one of them was in Swedish. She was not old enough to understand what she was saying, but she leaned into her parents' arms at night and said words that calmed and soothed.

Many of us have learned table graces. We may not know God, but we give God thanks for everything from spaghetti to fried clams. It works. Just as there is not one way to be a friend or lover, there is no number-one, bestselling way to pray—no single prayer for grace, grief or salvation. We can actually come into the mysterious places of God not having it all planned out.

You can pray as the first or last thing in your day, in public over a meal or in private. You can pray in words, but it is not necessarily better than settling into the arms of Jesus in silence. You can sing your prayers, or run or dance your prayers. The point is to enter the circle of love and trust with God. Sometimes prayers come easily. Floods of words tumble out. Sometimes prayer is hard. Words dry up.

BORROWING AND LENDING PRAYERS

When you ache after God but don't know what to say, consider borrowing and lending prayers. Ride the words of others who have opened their hearts to heaven. We find prayers in the Bible that voice our hearts: in Psalms, Lamentations, and the prayers of Hannah, Mary, Jesus and Paul. We borrow from St. Patrick, St. Francis, Teresa of Ávila, Ted Loder, the Book of Common Prayer, *The Divine Hours*. It all counts.

Adele's go-to-sleep prayer is from the Book of Common Prayer. It has tucked millions of believers in bed. "Keep watch, dear Lord, with those who work, or watch, or weep this night, and give your angels charge over those who sleep. Tend the sick, Lord Christ; give rest to the weary, bless the dying, soothe the suffering, pity the afflicted, shield the joyous; and all for your love's sake. Amen."[6] Sometimes Adele shortens it, "Lord, keep, watch, tend, bless and soothe. Amen."

Tracey often clings to the first segment of the Prayer of St. Francis of Assisi,

Lord, make me an instrument of your peace;

Where there is hatred, let me sow love;

Where there is injury, pardon;

Where there is error, truth;

Where there is doubt, faith;

Where there is despair, hope;

Where there is darkness, light;

And where there is sadness, joy.

It helps her remember her purpose in moments of life-cracking chaos.

During a hard season, for 365 days Adele borrowed Jeremiah's blaming, kicking and screaming lament. "I am the [one] who has seen affliction. . . . [God] has driven me away and made me walk in darkness rather than light. . . . He has besieged me and surrounded me with bitterness and hardship. . . . Even when I call out or cry for help, he shuts out my prayer" (Lamentations 3). Scripture offers us so many places like this. When your own words get wedged deep in the throat, pray Hannah's lament (1 Samuel 1) or Mary's *Magnificat* (Luke 1:46-55) or one of the psalms.

PRAY AS YOU CAN, NOT AS YOU CAN'T

Some prayers come with feeling and faith. Others come with doubt: "Lord, I believe. Help my unbelief." It's okay to let our prayers reflect our anger, guilt and disappointment with God. Unexpressed feelings do not slip past God. They bubble up. They fester in our lives. Step into praying as you can rather than fretting about the prayers you cannot offer. Emilie Griffin puts it like this: "We find ourselves set free not by doing but undoing, by relenting and being just who we are and who God means us to be."[7]

God does not keep a watch to time our prayers or measure the spirituality of our words. In the night when we lie awake worrying about an illness, a parent, child or spouse, or covering the bills, praying as we *can* might sound like, "God, here it is. I'd stop worrying if I could, but I'm a wreck right now. Can you help me calm down?" Real. True. Honest. When we remember a friend who is suffering, it can be enough to say, "God, Jan. God, Jan." God cares about Jan, and us, and the fact that we ache for friends like Jan. It all counts.

It doesn't matter what technique you use. Just make some space to nestle against God's side and sooner or later grace will come to let the selfish go. Just like children who beg for a cuddle and snuggle at bedtime, we can come to God the same way and be met by the Holy.

THOSE UNANSWERED PRAYERS

Eventually, no matter how much or hard we pray, we crash headlong into the silence of God and seemingly unanswered prayer. "God, where did you go?" "Why are bad things happening to really good people?" It turns out God is not obligated to answer prayers according to our timetable and satisfaction, which makes billions of us angry and achy.

Still it is so easy to give God directions about what we need and how life should go down. We pray to have friends, for health, protection or a Pottery Barn–looking life. When we don't get these things we may pray harder or enlist everyone else's prayers—amassing a big gang to go to God for us (which can be trusting numbers more than God).

We cannot tie happiness to an outcome rather than to God. Cherish the Giver and not just the gifts you want. Yes, we can pray for what we want. Jesus did: "Father, if you are willing, take this cup from me" (Luke 22:42). But Jesus also was more attached to God's will than to his own agenda, "Yet not as I will, but as you will" (Matthew 26:39). When we are truly after God's will (a nearly impossible feat) our happiness is no longer tied to one answer. Our well-being is attached to God and God alone. On the cross Jesus prayed, "My God, my God, why have you forsaken me?" (Matthew 27:46). In some ways it sounds like despair. But when we call someone "my Amy" or "my Lynda," aren't we actually in the heart of intimacy? For Jesus, intimacy with God held as he detached himself from what he wanted and clung to "my God." Silent cries, wordless waiting or banging away on heaven's door, it's all part of a relationship with the One who is good and beyond us and our control. The sea of prayer is large enough to float everything from ecstasy to betrayal. God is in it all.

SHOW UP FOR GOD

Proverbial wisdom says that to succeed at being a human being you must:

1. Show up

2. Pay attention

3. Tell the truth without denial or blame

4. Not be attached to the outcome

This sounds like prayer. Each step is intentional and practical and makes us more present to God.

Show up! God is present in the middle of illness, busyness and ache even when we aren't present to ourselves. You can meet God as you scroll through your Twitter feed or commute to work. You don't need a perfect place or time. Be present to where you are, to who you are and to the reality that God is with you.

Pay attention. Identify where you most experience God's presence— is it when you lie in bed at the end of a day, sing, hug your family, study, break bread with friends or worship with God's people? Take in the details. Where does the veil between heaven and earth seem thinnest to you? Go there. Go to that single place and wait. Let a few shreds of heaven surround you.

Tell the truth. Dare to say, "So even if I don't get what I want and the worst happens . . ." Even if this makes you obnoxious, blaming and on edge, be honest with God. Tell the truth about your failures, anxieties and doubts. Truth builds relationships. Without truth we will never see our blind spots or recognize our goodness.

Detach from the outcome. God is not some cosmic vending machine or Albus Dumbledore. Yet sometimes our prayers are so riddled with expectations about how God should answer that it feels like standing at the roulette table. I recently changed a longtime prayer for someone because my happiness was completely tied up in one outcome. I was so attached to my agenda I couldn't see anything God was doing. So instead of praying for my will to be done I began to pray for this person to see the goodness of God that was all around them. That even if the goodness did not look like I thought it should, it would still be seen. I started praying that God would work in what *was* for their good, their growth and God's glory. Prayers like this bring God's will and not our own.

We'd add a fifth item to this list of what is essential to succeeding at prayer life:

Gratitude. Give thanks for something. Seek out one slim, little glint of grace. Like a dandelion shoving itself through cracked asphalt, good can emerge from concrete places. Gratitude (even if through gritted teeth) changes our perspective and gives us hope. As we practice giving thanks the Holy Spirit rewires those complaining fight-or-flight neural pathways. Prayers of thanksgiving keep us connected to the heartbeat of love and life.

Foreboding as the way ahead may be, when we risk the goodness of God we can resonate with Dame Julian of Norwich (1342–1416) when she wrote, "All shall be well, and all shall be well, and all manner of thing shall be well."[8]

JOURNAL AND PRACTICE

1. Consider crafting a short prayer that is easy to recall and recite throughout your day. Breath prayer is one way to talk to God in a simple "one liner" format. To craft a breath prayer, take a moment to slow down and notice the pace of your own breath. Then, take an attribute of God that feels significant to where you are on your journey and make that into the first part of a statement that you breathe in. Next, finish the statement by adding your petition to God to the first half. For example: "God of justice, grant me peace." Or, "Lover of my soul, help me live with grace." Or, "Good Shepherd, carry my lost lamb."

2. Consider using some of the templates available through social media to help you get a framework for prayer. We are not suggesting that you actually pray via social media, but most of us are in these formats daily. If you were to limit your words to God (like the 140 characters of Twitter), what would you say? Snap pictures and populate an Instagram feed with images that move you to prayer—images of people you love or situations that either give you hope or frustrate you. Consider using these images as a sort of prayer journal.

3. If you are visual or crafty, collage your prayers and desires before God with glue and scissors. Gather materials and a notebook. Cut and paste words, photos, pictures. What happens when you approach God this way? Check out *Praying in Color* by Sybil MacBeth.

4. Consider where you feel connected with God: in nature, holding a friend's baby or grandbaby, running, in quiet, reading the Word, sitting with friends at table, in bed, etc. Be attentive to God. Open your heart in that moment. This, too, is prayer.

5. Create a timeline or list of the "history" of your prayer life (even if you feel like you've rarely ever prayed). What were the situations in which you offered prayers? Were they times of stress, chaos or joy? How have your prayers grown, diminished, changed or evolved over time?

6. If you could pray along the lines of Anne Lamott's *Help, Thanks, Wow*, what three words would you choose? Take time to choose three exclamations that help craft your prayers, and then write a series of prayers that fit under each word. Use these prayers as they come to you throughout your day and week.

7. The psalms are a glimpse into David's "journal" and journey with God. Choose a few psalms (or if you're ambitious, several psalms) to journal through. Read your psalm and write down any words

that "light up" for you, give you pause or tug at an emotion you are carrying. What is the conversation you want to have with God that this psalm opens up for you? Write your conversation with God in your journal.

8. List your prayers for people and the world in your journal. Reflect on God's desire around each of your requests. What does God want to happen in the world and in the people around you? Notice how God answers your prayers. Sometimes the answer is wait, or no. And those are answers too. Journal around your prayer requests and what God is doing in you as you pray.

PART THREE

True Influence

10

TRUE WISDOM

Drawn by eons of collective memory.

ADELE CALHOUN AND
TRACEY BIANCHI

For two years our family had the best babysitter. Truly. On Brandy's first day she came skipping through our door—well rested, mid-twenties, hair all shiny and bouncy, perfect white teeth and tanned skin. So pretty. So hip. So peppy. I gave her the low-down on nap schedules and snack preferences for three children then went to grab my laptop and glanced in the mirror. Yikes. (Note: middle-aged women should not look in the mirror when a twenty-year-old is in their house.) The litany began: *When did my eyelids start to sag? Gosh, I look really washed out. When do we rename freckles "age spots"? When did my boobs start pointing straight down?*

Tina Fey once quipped that what turning forty meant for her was, "I need to take my pants off as soon as I get home. I didn't used to have to do that. But now I do."[1] It was 8:00 a.m. and I already could not wait to get my pants off. They were too tight and I was too tired to exercise.

At each stage of life we join a club with members-only privileges.

There are inside jokes, dress-code restrictions, dues and fees required. We may choose to flash our membership card with pride, or we may pretend we don't belong to that club. My dad is sixty-six and claims he's never seen his AARP card. Working on this chapter we noticed that up to this point we have named our life stages but neither of us has actually told you how old we are. Why leave it out? The truth is Tracey is forty-one and Adele is sixty-five. There. We said it.

Why was that so hard? In some cultures age is a benefit and honored. But in ours age dubs you irrelevant and invisible. Which, in turn, hides the true you.

SEASONS

We both live in parts of the country that boast seasons with great splendor and majesty. We don't criticize fall when its leaves drop. Instead, we celebrate the rash beauty of blazing colors and fat fields that all but burst before the season ends. We enjoy when spring blooms fully and do not criticize her for dropping petals that give way to the dark green of summer. We happily plant saplings and hug ancient beech trees. We honor their vulnerability, marveling at the beauty each season brings. Why can't we do the same with ourselves?

We are splendid creatures, vulnerable, and moving through seasons. Children don't realize this is happening—always happy to be a little bit bigger. But at some point this all changes. We rue the move from summer to fall or fall to winter. We grasp, sometimes desperately, to what was.

Honoring the "true you" as we age, at any age, means:

1. We are ready to let go.

2. We are vulnerable.

3. We are beautiful.

4. We are present.

These four things show up differently in our lives depending on our current life stage, struggles, triumphs and context.

LETTING GO

When I (Adele) was thirty-four an older friend told me, "It's never too early to learn the lessons of letting go. They prepare you for the stage when all that is left is letting go." That was a total downer. I was in the amassing stage of life, accumulating a mortgage, a job, vehicles, connections, friends, stuff and activities for children. My life was about providing, provisioning and organizing. I wanted to have, get, do and stockpile memories to paste into scrapbooks. Life was full. Letting go was for old people.

Yet letting go doesn't descend on you one day in the form of an empty nest or assisted living. Letting go starts invisibly. Small losses of attrition add up slowly over time. You are in half a dozen weddings, but not your own. Baby showers become a source of grief rather than joy. You don't get invited to the party. You get passed over for a promotion. You blow out your knee. The losses can come fast, yet we can receive them in spite of a culture that teaches us to brace ourselves against them.

This fight against letting go is a multinational economic enterprise. We join the gym (again) and gather up lotions, potions, Atkins, South Beach, kale salad and Botox to help us look young and relevant. Nora Ephron, with her wry sense of humor, captures the angst of transitions in *I Feel Bad About My Neck.* She writes,

> I feel bad about my neck. Truly I do. If you saw my neck, you might feel bad about it too, but you'd probably be too polite to let on. . . . Every so often I read a book about age, and whoever's writing it says it's great to be old. It's great to be wise and sage and mellow; it's great to be at the point where you understand just what matters in life. I can't stand when people say things

like this. What can they be thinking? Don't they have necks? Aren't they tired of compensatory dressing?[2]

I (Adele) resonate with Nora. My youth has been ambushed by a body that won't cooperate. If I go without makeup people ask, "Are you feeling ok?" Even my five-year-old great-nephew told me, "Aunt Adele, you might want to put some lipstick on." Really! My days as a low maintenance gal are over. To avoid the "naked truth" I accessorize, camouflage and begrudgingly sustain wardrobes in two different sizes, trying to remember the gift of another birthday is life sweet life—not just pounds!

Birthdays can be so dramatic. At twenty-nine, thirty-nine or seventy-nine we can boast about our connection to that younger decade, "I'm still in my fifties." It's so hard to let go of the decade and move on. Just as Adele learned about letting go from a friend, I learned from her. As we let go, there is loss—loss of our youth, plans, hopes, dreams, children, jobs, etc. It's not all bad; we gain memories and wisdom and enlarge our hearts. Still sometimes these seem to pale in comparison to skinny jeans and the freedom of youth.

Letting go is at the heart of life, beckoning us to embrace the way our true you changes rather than combat it. Our egos want to cling like cats. We clutch on to old stuff—stuff we have to pay to store. I (Tracey) am given to fits of panic or a funk of catastrophic thinking about a future with less than we have now. I (Adele) toss and turn and stress about how to downsize, where to live and how to pay for the years of retirement. No one avoids letting go.

Adele's next move means letting go of rooms and collections: art, books, photo albums, dishes, antiques and toys that don't have grandkids to rescue them. I don't like when she talks about "the great letting go." When she says, "One day we will have to lay ourselves or someone we love into the arms of Jesus and let go," I want to vomit. But I know she is right. Every letting go that happens before this—

the letting go of school, your parents' home, your first job, salary, independence, car keys, dexterity, flexibility, great legs—prepares us for "the great letting go." It makes us feel so exposed.

BE VULNERABLE

I remember feeling shocked when I learned about the indignities and vulnerabilities of Roman crucifixions. Crucifixion was meant to be excruciating and humiliating. People were hung up naked, exposed, vulnerable, pinned down for all to see. Jesus didn't even have a little hospital drape across his body at his crucifixion. The God who came in person, who hallowed all flesh and bone, didn't call ten thousand angels to deliver him from the vulnerability of being beaten to death. As people mocked and thieves argued and soldiers gambled, Jesus wore his naked skin for all to see. Talk about vulnerable. Talk about unfair. Talk about the "great letting go." Naked he came, and naked he went.

Naked bodies remind us of how vulnerable we are to abrupt, unexpected and traumatic ambushes. The sweet skin of babies and thin bruised skin of the aged tell intimate stories of letting go. A friend's six-year-old gets meningitis. A sixteen-year-old faces chemotherapy. A mom with young kids is diagnosed with MS or ALS. Not all vulnerabilities follow a logical pattern of age. Letting go can be thrust on us at any stage. We are always at the mercy of our finitude. A friend recently reminded me how skin-to-skin contact with both the very young and the very old can be almost transcendent and very hard to describe. The young physically throb with the promise of life, fresh and direct from the hand of God. The old physically have the proof that we were meant for more. All of their living and loving is preparation to return again to God—it is not the end. They are headed back to God's hand and the embrace of their true you in the eternity of God's story.

We have choices about how we weather the vulnerabilities of letting go—choices that embrace or deny our true life stage. When being ill, impaired or aged makes us invisible, we can bear this "naked" sign of vulnerability with Jesus. When paralysis or an autoimmune disorder leaves once-limber legs limp, we still have choices. No, we are not hanging naked on a cross—but we can lose our life to find it. Jesus' nakedness reminds me I won't be taking any stuff with me at the great letting go. I can accept my vulnerability and lean into the million little letting goes ahead of me. When we embrace the vulnerabilities and all the letting go, we can stay true to our truest selves.

BE BEAUTIFUL

When we were young, school-age kids we missed that our bodies were lithe and strong. My seven-year-old can all but wrap his legs around his head. As women age into even middle school we begin to fixate on the beauty we are lacking, and by middle age we miss that we are still alive to offer commentary! Wrinkles and scars hold stories about the true you, who God made. There is aching beauty for those who have eyes to see.

Jesus said very little about aging and died probably in his mid-thirties. But he did say to Peter: "'Very truly I tell you, when you were younger you dressed yourself and went where you wanted; but when you are old you will stretch out your hands, and someone else will dress you and lead you where you do not want to go.' Jesus said this to indicate the kind of death by which Peter would glorify God. Then he said to him, 'Follow me!'" (John 21:18-19).

"When you were younger you dressed yourself." My (Adele's) mother dressed herself until someone else did. The loss of this simple freedom was excruciating. But hard as it was for my mother to let this go, it was a gift to me. Each time I buttoned her sweater or helped her get dressed I remembered all the buttons she had buttoned for me. One day it may be your daughter, niece or best friend buttoning your sweater. We all let go for one another.

Paul writes, "Therefore we do not lose heart. Though outwardly we are wasting away, yet inwardly we are being renewed day by day" (2 Corinthians 4:16). There is a place inside us that is being transformed "with ever-increasing glory" (2 Corinthians 3:18). It is as if an unexplainable, beautiful part of us is getting newer and more Godlike every year. It reminds me of St. Augustine, who said, "God is younger than all else." Incredible.

Day after day we send who we are out there into the world. We play with friends, go to school, run a marathon, work a job, raise a family, and may even be blessed enough to hold our grandchildren. Every season holds beauty. Each stage is a gift that ripples out across the surface of this world. Even in tragedy and trauma, beauty and grace hide out. We may not see it in the moment, but putting our life out there is to trust that just as God brought beauty out of Jesus' vulnerable and tortured body, so God can bring beauty out of our wounds and ashes too.

BE PRESENT

It is easy to make the present moment a crack between nostalgia or regrets about the past and anxieties about the future. It takes embracing the true you to live what actually is, to be fully present and in the moment. The oddly famed character Ferris Bueller said, "Life moves pretty fast; if you don't stop and look around once in a while, you could miss something."

Every age and every stage—receive it, accept it, live it, own it, work it. It's your one, unrepeatable, beautiful life. When we value the stories we have been gifted to carry, rather than the way we look as we deliver them, we can release our literal death grip on life and receive the life we have been given. Let go and choose life.

What follows is an inexact, unscientific conversation on the stages of a woman's life and how she might live the beauty, vulnerability and "letting go" of each season. Consider each and what it says to your true you. Do you resonate with, fight against or deny any of the following? You may do so for good reason, but consider what each pulls up in you.

Life Stage	Living the Season
Childhood	*Beauty*–unselfconscious enthrallment with life's fullness and glory *Vulnerability*–great sensitivity and need on all levels *Letting go*–learning that delayed gratification can lead to something more *Temptation*–selfishness
Adolescence	*Beauty*–physical vitality and stamina and character formation: internalizing (or not) of faith beliefs, obedience, agency *Vulnerability*–excruciating self-consciousness and relational angst *Letting go*–of dependence on parents to explore the true you *Temptation*–FOMO (fear of missing out)
Young adult	*Beauty*–owning potentials, competency and abilities *Vulnerability*–to failure and relational transition and angst *Letting go*–of home and reliance on immediate family *Temptation*–indulging appetites
Thirty-something	*Beauty*–gracefully shouldering responsibility for others *Vulnerability*–exhaustion and over-reaching one's limits *Letting go*–laying down sleep, money, time, etc., for the sake of someone else or career *Temptation*–materialism, control, competition, ingratitude
Midlife	*Beauty*–growing productivity and self-awareness about motives, persona, defenses, desires, losses, etc. *Vulnerability*–to materialism, FOMO, competition *Letting go*–of control, aging parents, children who leave home *Temptation*–refusing to let go; powering up and pretending you are still twenty

Life Stage	Living the Season
Sixtyish	*Beauty*–of experience, wisdom and self-forgetfulness
	Vulnerability–around issues of health and how long to stay "in the game"
	Letting go–empty nest, job, retirement, grandchildren, downsizing, etc.
	Temptation–to rigidity and resisting change
Senior	*Beauty*–wisdom of the soul shines out
	Vulnerability–to physical, emotional, mental and relational loss
	Letting go–of decades of hard-won independence
	Temptation–to become bitter, hang on and refuse to let go

JOURNAL AND PRACTICE

1. Notice the scars, tattoos, freckles, birthmarks or any other marks on your body. Consider the stories they tell. What do they reveal about you?

2. Do a body scan. What parts of your body feel tense, tight or tired? What story is your body telling you? How do you need to respond?

3. When and how have you thanked God for the body you have been given? A body that can think or dance, hands that can cook dinner, give high fives and hugs? Write a list of gratitudes for your body.

4. Consider making a collage of your story. Clip photos and images that illustrate who you have become over time. Do your collage with a friend and share stories with one another.

5. Look over the list of ages and stages. Take each age/stage and consider the four things listed (beauty, vulnerability, letting go and temptation) at each life stage. How did these things affect your sense of your true you right now?

6. What has been your favorite life stage thus far? Why? What did you learn about yourself and God in that stage? How has it changed your story?

7. What has been your hardest life stage so far? What did you learn about yourself and God in that stage? (It may be the same stage that was your favorite.)

8. Name a person in each life stage that has been an icon to you of living their story well. What can you learn from them? Consider writing a thank-you note to her. What might you say?

9. What "letting go" is at the heart of your life right now? What do you want to say to God about it?

11

JUSTICE FOR ALL

I have more. Please take some.

ADELE CALHOUN AND
TRACEY BIANCHI

Every morning during grade school I (Adele) put my hand to my heart and blithely said the Pledge of Allegiance—"one nation, under God, indivisible, with liberty and justice for all." I was young and had no idea that I had a hand in bringing justice for all. I now know differently, and I feel both adamant and guilty about it. Part of the true you inside each of us yearns to bring about the true self in others. Even in the smallest of ways, a warm smile or gentle hug, we are harbingers of justice when we allow ourselves to be.

When my (Adele's) daughter, Annaliese, was nine our family went to the Dominican Republic to help build a house. We slept on the floor of a school, bathed at a standing water pipe, and worked (and played) side by side with local families. We folded into the community. About an hour after we returned home Annaliese handed me her pink backpack and Cabbage Patch doll. "Mama! Send these to my friend Vicki in the D. R."

I responded, "Are you sure? These are your favorites."

Annaliese solemnly nodded. "Vicki doesn't have a doll or a backpack. I want her to have mine."

I (Tracey) had a similar experience with my oldest son as we sifted through toy bins in the basement searching for items to donate. I was looking for the "no longer played with" junk that seemed easy to discard when Danny came to me with his most prized Nerf gun. "Here, Mom, let's give this to someone." It was a new toy, a bit expensive, and I cringed, assuming (like a selfish moron) that we would need to replace it.

"Oh buddy, are you sure you want to give that one up? That's one of your good toys."

"Well, Mom, you said we were giving these to kids in need, and everyone needs a good Nerf gun."

It was not "should" or "ought" that moved Danny and Annaliese to generosity that surpassed our own. For a gleaming little moment in time they felt solidarity with someone else. Their sense of being united with another child made them act to even things out. They wanted to sacrifice, share and simplify. Their willingness to give their best stuff made both of us feel glad and guilty. Oh, the guilt of good.

We both care about and talk about justice often, but actually living justice gets complicated—and guilt can be the underlying mantra. Have we really done enough to even things out? There is always more we *could* do; after all, compared to the rest of the world most of us have it pretty good. Even if we've struggled to link life together between paychecks, lacked money for healthcare or not payed the rent for a month, most of us have been warm and fed enough. Should we be grateful? or mad? or scared? or all of these?

JUSTICE ISSUES ARE COMPLEX

Many women (even in the good old US of A) suffer injustices like slavery, trafficking, domestic abuse and not earning a living wage. In some parts of the world girls are attacked with acid or sexually assaulted for simply walking to school. Flip open your laptop and take in a whole world of hurt. The Middle East is teetering on the verge of anarchy. North Korea festers like an open wound. Sub-Saharan Africa is awash in refugees. No corner of the globe is absolutely safe, including our own. No family is completely immune from the wildcards of earthquakes, favoritism, prejudice and terrorism. Statistics for 2014 are mind blowing:

- Twenty-one million people are enslaved.

- Anywhere from four to twenty-seven million people are trafficked each year. 70% are female and 50% are children.

- Human trafficking is a thirty-two billion dollar per year venture.[1]

- A billion children live in poverty, and twenty-two thousand die each day due to poverty.[2]

- Twenty-three percent of children in the United States live in poverty.[3]

- Thirty thousand children die each day from preventable diseases.[4]

Listing global injustices becomes burdensome and then simply numbing. We murmur, "It's not okay to let this happen on our watch." Yet, after we say this, most of us retreat to a need-induced anesthesia that numbs us when we are overwhelmed by this world. It takes a willingness to work through some inner tensions if we want to bring our true selves to stand for and in solidarity with others. Meanwhile,

- We make resolutions to serve more but ache for time alone.

- We take a short rant at human atrocities yet pour daily energy into raging at traffic.

- We lament the changing climate while filling up an SUV.

- We have enough, yet shop for more.

- We beg, borrow and sometimes steal resources from future generations while hailing the promise of the future for them.

Women often feel conflicted—both active and passive, motivated and defeated, guilty and blessed. We're torn between "I'm just one person" and "every bit we give counts." How we hold these tensions of our own comfort and the struggle of others is part of the true you that we all must wrestle with.

HOLDING THE TENSION

It's not easy to make sense of a beautiful world where horrific catastrophes happen. Most of us are relatively safe. Others are not. The weight-loss industry rakes in twenty billion dollars annually while others starve.[5] We vaccinate our children while others die of curable diseases. We stash an extra jacket that matches just one outfit in a closet while others shiver.

It's not wrong to have love, a full belly and healthy children. It's quite natural to focus on the needs of those closest to us. To draw our arms tightly around them and do our best for them is second nature. But what about everybody else? What about Jesus' injunction to "love your neighbor as yourself" (Mark 12:31; Matthew 22:39)? What about the second greatest commandment after loving God?

Is there a balance between what is on my plate and what is on the world's plate? Is praying for a neighbor enough? And who exactly is my neighbor, anyway? Does caring for a neighbor mean entering the political fray, emptying our savings accounts or checking every product we buy with the "Fair Trade Finder" app on our smartphones? Does the thought of doing this give you a migraine? When conversations about justice are linked to phrases like "compassion fatigue" and "burnout," we know it's complicated. Yet each day we must choose where to invest our time, prayers and finances. Does God have some expectations of how we are to do that?

BIBLICAL JUSTICE

Justice is not a side issue to God. In the Old Testament, God's prophets are literally out to re-create a world where the poor, oppressed, voiceless and powerless experience the justice and shalom of God. Prophets wear God's heart on their sleeves, brooding over an earth gone to rack and ruin. Their voices challenge and at times berate God's people to remake what human selfishness and disobedience has destroyed.

- "Learn to do right; seek justice. Defend the oppressed. Take up the cause of the fatherless; plead the case of the widow" (Isaiah 1:17).

- "This is what the LORD Almighty said: 'Administer true justice; show mercy and compassion to one another. Do not oppress the widow or the fatherless, the foreigner or the poor. Do not plot evil against each other'" (Zechariah 7:9-10).

- "This is what the LORD says: Do what is just and right. Rescue from the hand of the oppressor the one who has been robbed. Do no wrong or violence to the foreigner, the fatherless or the widow, and do not shed innocent blood in this place" (Jeremiah 22:3).

- "Rejoice with those who rejoice; mourn with those who mourn. Live in harmony with one another. Do not be proud, but be willing to associate with people of low position. Do not be conceited. Do not repay anyone evil for evil. Be careful to do what is right in the eyes of everyone. If it is possible, as far as it depends on you, live at peace with everyone" (Romans 12:15-18).

- "What does the LORD require of you? To act justly and to love mercy and to walk humbly with your God" (Micah 6:8).

Even the Ten Commandments (Exodus 20) reveal God's concern for human flourishing:

- right to life (you shall not murder)

- right to property and resources (you shall not steal)

- right to rest (keeping the Sabbath)

- right to home (you shall not commit adultery)

- right to reputation (you shall not give false testimony)

A KINGDOM OF CHANGE

God cares about human dignity and aches when justice is so perverted that the poor have no redress. The Bible should spark revolution in each of us. Though the Bible—like other religious writings from history—affirms authority, it also elevates and prizes the value of the weak and the broken, the needy and downtrodden. It lifts up the smallest and makes them the magnificent. If we really lived like this was true it would be an absolute affront to social systems both then and now. It would make us advocates for systemic change.

The clearest evidence of God's passion for the broken is when God came in person, in Jesus, and took a stand of solidarity with the poor and oppressed. Jesus descended through the birth canal of a powerless young woman into a family without resources or status or a home in a swanky suburb. Jesus' message irritated the elite. He taught that the "meek will inherit the earth" and that peacemakers will be called "children of God" (Matthew 5). He preached (like the prophets before him) the coming of a new creation and the remaking of the world. Jesus called this new creation the kingdom of God, and he invited his disciples to help him bring in this new paradigm. Clearly, this vision of a new way of relating to one another was received as an obnoxious affront. Jesus was framed by false witnesses, tried and abused by a kangaroo court, judged for crimes he didn't commit, and condemned and executed without just protocols. Jesus tasted the lash and nail of injustice in solidarity with humankind in order to mend and renew all creation.

It is theologically sound to say that the Trinity is in solidarity with human beings for the remaking of all creation. Father, Son and Holy Spirit are not uniform; they are distinct from one another. Yet they unite in love to rescue and restore creation. Each seeks the good of the other, giving themselves completely to love. This relational love and oneness among distinct persons of the Trinity is the model for and the heart of justice.

AFFLUENZA

Like a carbon-monoxide leak we cannot smell or see, we constantly breathe in the toxic message that we need and deserve more. Achieving and accumulating more is the norm. Some call the condition "affluenza," a contagion infecting people with ruthless competitiveness and an addiction to shopping. Affluenza blinds us to the fact that amassing exacerbates systems of injustice. One-upping my neighbor creates deeper chasms between rich and poor. As affluenza spreads we become immune to the inequities of the world—a world that really does have enough to go around. It escapes us that we are more the same than different. This pandemic grieves the Creator and undermines the divine vision of a new creation.

Justice, like a tuning fork, sets our hearts to resonate with others. It enlarges our true you to see what is good and to seek the common good. When my good is your good we are one with the common good. When we don't compete for resources we are in solidarity. One humanity. One shared human experience. The Trinity "ones" with people without advocates, without freedom, without opportunity, without plenty. Justice is always about loving the other as yourself.

Justice implicates me. My unique context, gifts, talents, resources, time, finances and location can serve me and mine, or others, or the inequitable system. I can partner with God to create cities that are more equal and fair, or I can create my own empire. No, it's not just an either-or equation. Loving others includes loving myself. We must frame a both-and solution—a solution where both ends and means serve the flourishing of others, a solution that realizes when freedoms are at stake and that tenderness, kindness, patience, forgiveness, perseverance, presence and sacrifice matter. Justice is not about forcing people to do right things.

WHO ARE THE SLAVES?

It's not just the poor who are oppressed or enslaved. Some people are slaves to an unjust system; others are enslaved (addicted) to wielding power. Sometimes oppressive systems crush through outside forces. But sometimes, half in love with our own self-destruction, we give inner lies and addictions free rein to encroach on our freedom to flourish. When our ability to feel unique or powerful receives an affront we act out against others. There are many ways to be in thrall to "this little life of mine."

The world needs people prepared to enter the fray with God's own self-donating love. A friend who is a professor at Harvard Business School told me (Adele) a story he heard when Mother Teresa spoke on campus. After her lecture a question came from a young woman, "I so much respect the work you do to help the sick and the poor. My friends and I are equally passionate about helping those in need and have spent the last several years doing so. But I find it difficult to hear your insistence of bringing Jesus into the discussion. I do not need Jesus to want to do the right thing."

Mother Teresa paused and gently asked, "How old are you?"

The young woman responded, "Twenty-six."

Mother Teresa smiled. "I'm nearly ninety. I've been doing this my entire life. Try loving, serving and caring for the poor as long as I have, and then tell me you don't need Jesus."

Anyone can do good. But shouldn't those of us who know we are held in the arms of God's love be free enough to hand over our agendas and risk that we have enough? Free people don't spend an entire lifetime accumulating and replacing stuff. They find a way to stand in solidarity with others so that everyone can flourish. They have the back of the oppressed rather than support lifestyles and economic policies that stab them in the back. It's virtually impossible to stand in solidarity with people and then compete for the largest piece of the comfort pie. Solidarity means loving my neighbor as myself.

STANDING IN SOLIDARITY

I (Adele) recently went to a justice conference and participated in a game that wrecked me. The group of attendees was divided in half and each person was handed five cards that listed out freedoms:

1. Control over your sexuality

2. Opportunity to make your own decisions

3. Physical safety

4. Respect from others

5. Religious freedom

Once the cards were doled out, my group was told we had power to take cards away from the other group. We were told to mingle, meet people in the other group and eventually ask for one of their cards. The game was unnerving. I did not want to be the one with the most cards at the end of the game, so I would meet people but not ask for their cards. I stood off to the side and refused to engage, leaving me with five cards at the end of the game.

The leader debriefed the game and asked the group without cards what it felt like to lose their freedoms. She asked those with a pile of cards what it felt like to take cards away. I sat there all smug. I had not competed to win. I was not complicit in stomping on the freedom of others. I raised my hand and said that I had refused to take any cards. Then someone from the group that lost freedoms raised a hand and quipped, "Well, aren't you jolly nice?! Why didn't you try to get anyone else in your group to resist along with you?" Ouch. I had competed to be just but not to help others win or trump the system. I practiced some passive resistance, but it never occurred to me to stand in solidarity with the others, or for that matter, to give any of my own cards away. My individualism, autonomy and self-determination remained intact. There was no show of solidarity.

This is how it is with many of us. We have the ability to fight oppressive systems and help restore freedom to people, and yet we fall short. We may even sit smugly on the side thinking we aren't complicit

with unjust systems. We aren't taking from the poor. We care, in fact—
but solidarity is care that sacrifices, lets go, comes down and enters
into the lot of another (like Jesus did). It's not enough to be "jolly nice"
to people. Nice does not lead to freedom or change. To bring God's
full, restorative hope to the world takes solidarity and sacrifice.
Progress in justice depends on someone reaching deep down for their
courage in the midst of fear and doubt.

Dr. Brene Brown once said,

> It is not a choice to be brave or afraid—truth is you are afraid
> and brave in every minute of the day. The choice you must make
> is one of comfort or courage—because these are mutually ex-
> clusive; there is nothing comfortable in courage. If you go into
> that arena you will get your *** kicked. Vulnerability is not about
> winning or losing, it is about showing up and letting ourselves
> be seen. . . . It is not weakness; it is the birthplace of creativity
> and innovation.[6]

SOLIDARITY WITH OTHER WOMEN

The Bible pulls us toward justice for others. It does not limit us to
advocating only on behalf of women. But our very gender uniquely
suits us to pray, groan, ache and act on behalf of the population we
represent. We who bear two X chromosomes feel solidarity giggling
with Amy Poehler and Tina Fey; we nod all the way through a book
by Nora Ephron. Whether single or married, moms or not moms,
professionals or students, we all share our femininity. We understand
what middle school, menopause and a culture obsessed with bust size
does to the female soul. One of the deep joys many of us celebrate
with our girlfriends is our visceral connection as females. This reso-
nance has spurred movements from the Red Hat Society and Girl
Scouts to Girl Rising, from Women Moving Millions to Mothers
Against Drunk Driving.

Women's voices have often pointed out inconvenient truths that bring persecution and abuse. Malala Yousafzai is a Pakistani teenager who has spoken out about a girl's right to get an education. On October 9, 2012, a gunman boarded Malala's school bus. He asked Malala her name, pointed a Colt 45 at her head and fired three shots. When Malala survived, the Taliban reiterated its intention to kill her. Threats have not stopped Malala from using her voice to speak up for the right of every child to receive an education. *Time* magazine for April 29, 2013, lists her as one of the one hundred most influential women in the world.

Laws can prohibit a woman's right to live her true you. Some societies limit the education that empowers and grows. Other cultures market different stories about a woman's value:

- Real women are a leggy size zero.
- Real women know their place.
- Real women serve their husbands without question.
- Real women don't draw attention to themselves.

Sometimes we internalize these messages so deeply that we are unaware of them. Sometimes we try to ignore the messages and close our mouths, shut our eyes and cap our pens in response. But there is always the possibility that we can stand in solidarity with Malala and thousands of other women who seek the good and flourishing of all women (and men).

In 2009, Nicholas D. Kristof and Sheryl WuDunn, a husband-and-wife team, published a Pulitzer Prize–winning book titled *Half the Sky: Turning Oppression into Opportunity for Women Worldwide.* This book can wreck you. It gives voice to voiceless women, making a remarkable case that the "paramount human rights problem of this century" is the brutality routinely inflicted on women and girls in much of the world.[7] Injustices against women often go unreported. But the realities of rape, torture, maiming, enslaving, abusing, silencing and repression are prevalent and growing. Our female souls grieve. If not for circumstance, that could be me, my daughter, my mother, my best friend. We feel deep in our bodies the uniquely female atrocities—atrocities that make us recoil in a way other injustices do not. This visceral nudge in our gut is nothing less than an invitation to move toward justice. It is an opportunity to repent of our indifference and take responsibility for some of what is wrong in this world.

Barbara Brown Taylor writes that repentance "calls whole communities to engage in the work of repair and reconciliation without ever forgetting their own culpability for the way things are."[8] Let's get up and put our shoulder to God's dream for a just world, and stand in solidarity with sisters worldwide.

We hesitate to give suggestions about how to engage justice issues, because there are literally thousands of ways, thousands of venues and thousands of causes. Nonetheless, here are some recommendations for priming the pump:

- Today borrow or buy *Half the Sky*. Read it and pass it on.

- Take a course on how to help a woman who is in an abusive home situation. Adele took a course with Hagar's Sisters (www.hagars sisters.org) that provided her with help and resources for women who confide in her.

- Introduce your children to the world of microfinance. Read *One Hen* by Katie Smith Milway and check out the very cool website www.onehen.org.

- Introduce your children to Nobel Peace Prize winner (2004) Wangari Maathai through her book *Trees of Peace* (Tracey loves this one because it speaks to environmental justice). Visit www .greenbeltmovement.org.

- We both have apps on our phones that scan products for fair-trade compliance. Fair Trade Finder and GoodGuide are both free.

- Explore what resources your community lacks. Is there any way you can help with this need?

- Re-evaluate how you spend discretionary income. Free up some money and plan how to invest it so others can flourish as you do.

- Share what you have. It doesn't have to be money. Give time, volunteer, write a blog, become a Big Sister.

- Take a look at the practices offered below.

JOURNAL AND PRACTICE

1. Invite some friends to watch all or parts of *Girl Rising* or the documentary *Half the Sky*. Spend time discussing what these videos brought up in you. Are there next steps you want to take individually or as a group?

2. Do some scouting to find out where the community you live is short on resources. Share your findings with a friend and pray. Is there any way you are being called to lend a hand? If you're not able to provide resources, are there other ways you can serve?

3. Look for ways to share what you have so others don't need to buy more. Consider sharing snow blowers, lawn mowers, sporting equipment, rides, children's clothing and toys, etc.

4. Practice a "buy nothing" day each week.

5. As you look at life with all its unfairness and inequality, what is your message to the world? What is in your heart to say? Write it out. Consider putting your message into a six-word story. What would it be?

6. If you could give anything you wanted to this world, what would you give? How can you give this in bits and pieces to the world around you?

12

TRUE IMAGE

Beautiful, powerful God.
Beautiful, powerful woman.

ADELE CALHOUN AND
TRACEY BIANCHI

∝∾

Recently I (Tracey) was standing on the driveway of a neighbor's house yammering away with other parents while our children played basketball. Seven elementary school boys threw elbows and grabbed for the ball while my daughter (the youngest at age five and the only girl) tried desperately to wrestle her way into the game.

After ten minutes she ran to me, exasperated and sobbing, "Mommy, I want to be a boy! Why can't I be a boy?"

"Honey, what is wrong? Why do you feel like you need to be a boy?" I asked, wincing at her lament.

"Because boys always get to play the sports; I want to play the sports!"

Now, to be fair, she was overlooked in that athletic moment not because of her gender but because of her age, and yet her solution unsettled me. She believed that she had been ousted from the game because she was female, and the fix was to become a boy. Never mind that of my three children (the other two are boys) my daughter has bottled up inside of her more natural athleticism than my boys combined. Never mind that she stood at my feet a sopping mess of sweat and effort, having more than once come close to prying the basketball from the hands of a fourth grader. Somewhere seeded in her heart was the belief that to have an equal shot at events, she'd best ditch her gender. Which is to say, she'd best ditch the very nature of God in her.

Women can have limited opportunities. I have heard women offer the same lament as my daughter, "Well, if I were a man they would have listened, responded or accepted." How did we get from the glory of creation where all were created equally in God's image, *imago Dei*, to a world where bearing the female part of God's image is seen as a burden or limitation?

IMAGE BEARERS

In many Christian circles we naively take in the notion that men are "more equal" than women. The very first page of our Bible tells us that the stories of men and women both matter: "Let us make humankind in our image, according to our likeness; and let them have dominion. . . . So God created humankind in his image, in the image of God he created them; male and female he created them" (Genesis 1:26-27 NRSV). In God's eyes we *all* shine with the likeness of divinity. Every inch of us is stamped with God's own "very good." To miss the value and equality of God's image in men and women can only grieve the Creator. No gender or body or race is profane; each person is sacred. None are less. No story is irrelevant.

You are one-of-a-kind amazing. God's purpose is for you to rule and take charge of creation. Adam *and* Eve were both empowered to make culture—to create something in this world. Power is to have agency to alter, enhance, change and protect God's world. God intends for us to have power. Adam and Eve were to apply their skill, wits and imagination to God's creation project so it could thrive and flourish. To ignore God's distribution of power skews it into something lopsided and toxic. Power is not a synonym for leadership or dominance.

There is power in being young and in being old. Power in being experienced. Power in speaking up. Power in words, skills, beauty and peace.

Every living thing has some sort of power—even bacteria can alter this world. The World Health Organization claims we are at a near crisis point in human history because antibiotics can no longer fight little bacteria.[1] The power given to women and men is the power to be the image of God in the world. It's an epic task—breathtaking and daunting. It is a call to your true you—a call to use your power to collaborate with God in making this world a "very good" place to be alive.

In Genesis 1 and 2 God hands a newly minted, extravagant and diverse world to human beings. The gift comes with a responsibility to unmask the image of God and rule. This means stewarding a world in which men and women of every culture and race can flourish in peace—a world where voices and talents are leveraged and each of us is brassy enough to be and bear the image of God.

REFLECTING OUR CREATOR

When we get this right, when love and justice, beauty and peace flourish in us, people catch a glimpse of who God is. God's good intentions toward planet earth are revealed in us. Consider genetics and all the times you have caught sight of a person and exclaimed, "She/ He is the spitting image of her/his mother!"

Bearing the beauty of God's image in the world is an active, not passive, trait. We do not simply sit around and wait to see how this all shakes out. We get to step up and own our holy DNA and the power given to us. For many years I did not realize my responsibility to "participate in the divine nature" (2 Peter 1:3-4). I abdicated, and it felt like obedience. I confused humility with responsibility for my gifts and call.

It was my (Adele's) husband, Doug, who kept telling me I was being irresponsible with my "dominion." If a neighbor kid could start a co-op, a sixteen-year-old girl stand up to the Taliban, and a nation elect a female head of state, then I had to take my true you seriously! I had to be attentive to how God designed me and intentional about my call to make the world flourish. I had to stop hiding out behind Doug. I had to take responsibility (as well as some hits) for the divine image in me.

This means women, who are image bearers, have to stop internalizing cultural messages like

- You don't belong at the table with men.
- You don't have anything to offer.
- Your opinions, thoughts and ideas are secondary.
- Your body matters more than your voice.
- You must blindly lay down your dreams, hopes and gifts.

It can be excruciating for women to step into God's creation mandate to rule, but it is part of our true you. Stories of women's exploits and lives are in short supply, snuffed out because they seem irrelevant to great events of history—a history written and remembered mainly by men. Many cultures continue this bias by hand-selecting boys for education and favoring men for places of power of influence. Living out our God-given image within these realities can be terrifying—especially when we consider the success rate.

EMBRACING OUR IMAGES

This is a tricky conversation, one that is often laced with agendas that stray wildly from God's desire that this world and all human beings flourish together. We are talking about billions of women and girls who lack advocates who care about the image of God in them. The BBC reports that there are twenty-one million slaves in this world, mostly female.[2] The image of God in them is dishonored. God's original trajectory and purpose was to create cultures and structures in which both men and women flourish.

Yes, it gets all messed up in Genesis 3 when Adam and Eve decide they want more power—power to control reality, power to be like God. The tragic irony was their inability to see that the fruit wouldn't give them anything better than they already had as image bearers. In fact the fruit skewed the balance of power and agency. It turned us all into control freaks who wrestle God and one another for our own way. It set men up to think that ruling over women was their job rather than a distorted consequence of sin (Genesis 3:16).

This shows up in a controversial, historical rabbinic prayer, "Blessed are you King of the Universe who has not made me a Gentile, a woman or a slave."[3] This prayer has been interpreted by Jewish scholars in two ways: as an indictment against women or as an invitation to own and celebrate who the rabbis were. You may be asking, how could this sexist-sounding prayer ever be a good thing?

If this prayer is a call for men to celebrate their own God-given gender, it must hold true that women are invited to do the same. I am happy to pray, "Thank you God that you did not make me a man." As both men and women celebrate who they are it is possible to reclaim the goodness of the divine image in all of us.

THE FULL IMAGE BEARER

We are both so grateful to live in a time and place where education, opportunity and blessing have come our way. But we have also seen firsthand how the valuing of men over women can come out directly or in slippery little ways. To point out the bias against women is not a rant. It is to feel compassion toward the daily reality of billions of women and girls. When a well-received author like Dorothy Sayers writes a book titled *Are Women Human?* we know even those with seemingly every opportunity still struggle to be received as full image bearers.[4] This same doubt echoes in a child's letter to God:

Dear God,

Are boys better than girls? I know you are one, but please try to be fair.

Love,

Sylvia[5]

It's so easy to absorb messages about our identity from culture, religion, parents, spouses, friends, children, teachers, bosses and so on. These voices (living and dead) can shout at us: *You're stupid. Girls are dippy. Drop some weight. How old are you?!* The messages are a wrecking ball through our chests. How many women cringe at the thought of themselves as beautiful, favored creatures? Shame becomes the narrative of who we are. It's ridiculously simple to focus on what is wrong with us. We wake up every day feeling we still have to prove who we are, regardless of past success or accolades. The woman who wanted to be married wonders what is wrong with her. Older women have no idea how they became invisible. The mom who chooses to work wrestles with the narrative that she does not care enough about her kids. The mom who opts to stay home wonders if her story has any value in the marketplace. No matter who you are, married, single, young, old, absorbing the myths is easier than embracing the true you—a divine image bearer.

PROJECTED IMAGES

So many of the obstacles we face in living as God's image bearers stem from images projected onto us by others or even ourselves. Seeing past these projections is not easy. I (Adele) once was told in a job interview, "You remind me of someone who gave me a hard time at my old job." Really? I was stunned. Could he get past his projection and actually see me? I have had terrible experiences with teachers, dentists and pastors, and I have received vicious hate mail that makes me so heartsick I want to curl up for a week. Left unchecked, I can project my bad experience onto every dentist, teacher and pastor, but eventually I have to get my teeth cleaned and check my email. The truth is my inbox is mostly filled with good words, but the sting of a jab far outlasts the warm fuzzies. To see people as God does, I have to shed my projections.

God is not confused by projections. Every one of us is favored, and God's love is written into our DNA. When Gabriel visited Mary he said, "Greetings, you who are highly favored! The Lord is with you" (Luke 1:28). Do you ever wake up in the morning feeling favored? Often we forget our divine image. I know a family with four siblings who constantly argue over who is the favorite. Each one thinks they are the favored one. In God's family, it's true; you are the favorite. God calls, births and treasures you (Deuteronomy 32:18; Isaiah 49:1; Psalm 139:15-16).

In many ancient creation myths, the gods create out of violence and bloodshed. In the Babylonian creation myth, the *Enuma Elish* (15 B.C.), the cosmos happens when Marduk slashes the dragon Tiamat's skull and pulls heaven and earth from her ribs. Her weeping eyes are said to be the source of the Tigris and Euphrates. Her tail the Milky Way. This is creation from death. The biblical story of creation is a departure from these myths and an historic novelty. The God of Israel creates a world based on love, where human beings are icons of God's own image.

- God loves sons and daughters equally and wholeheartedly: "I have loved you with an everlasting love" (Jeremiah 31:3). "Bring my sons from afar and my daughters from the ends of the earth—everyone who is called by my name, whom I created for my glory, whom I formed and made" (Isaiah 43:6-7).

- God births: "But now, like a woman in childbirth, I cry out, I gasp and pant" (Isaiah 42:13-14). "Everyone who believes that Jesus is the Christ is born of God" (1 John 5:1) and "flesh gives birth to flesh, but the Spirit gives birth to spirit" (John 3:6).

- God adopts: "In love he predestined us for adoption to sonship through Jesus Christ, in accordance with his pleasure and will" (Ephesians 1:4-5).

- God nurtures: "Can a mother forget the baby at her breast and have no compassion on the child she has borne? Though she may forget, I will not forget you!" (Isaiah 49:15).

- God comforts: "You will nurse and be carried on her arm and dandled on her knees. As a mother comforts her child, so will I comfort you" (Isaiah 66:12-13).

The God whom the Jews would not debase with an image—the God who is Spirit—relates to us in ways we can understand, like a good father *and* mother. When we project our own images of mother and father on God, we fail to receive these metaphors and the healing that they bring.

Biologically speaking it is women who give birth. God births and mothers us all (Deuteronomy 32:18). This biblical, feminine birthing metaphor describes how each of us arrives stamped with the love and likeness of God. God chose to birth and rear forgetful, annoying, odd, funny, vulnerable, miserable, beautiful and rebellious children. Projecting only male qualities onto God is an affront to God. Certainly, masculine pronouns and descriptors like "Father" are used to describe much of God's work in this world. But embracing the maternal image of God as well allows the image of God its fullest expression. To miss this is to miss that God's maternal care is not just a role but part of the divine image.

BIBLICAL IMAGES

Jesus compares himself to a mother hen longing to cuddle, nestle and protect her chicks: "How often I have longed to gather your children together, as a hen gathers her chicks under her wings, and you were not willing" (Matthew 23:37). Jesus also knows a mother's grief when children push love away, refuse to settle and rebel. Paul even writes of his love for the Galatians using birthing images: "I must go through the pain of giving birth to you all over again until Christ is formed in you" (Galatians 4:19 JB). The feminine is alive and well in God. The Catechism of the Roman Catholic Church (CCC 239) captured this by saying God's parental "tenderness can also be expressed by the image of motherhood, which emphasizes God's immanence, and the intimacy between Creator and creature."[6] Are we not, as Renita Weems suggests, who we are because some mother, somewhere, stooped down long enough that we might climb on her back and ride piggyback into the future?[7]

God's mother love is dauntless, like a mother bear deprived of her cubs (Hosea 13:8). We see this mother angst reflected in the tenacity of organizations like Mothers Against Drunk Driving, Mothers of the Plaza de Maya, the Girl Scouts, Women's Suffrage, Big Sister, The Global Women's Fund, The Hildegard Fund, and on it goes.

Let's celebrate God's mother love. When we protect, birth, feed, teach, discipline and nurture we are doing the same work God does. Let's live into the true image of God—male *and* female. God's image is a beautiful two-part creation. More and more researchers like Anita Williams Wooley of Carnegie Mellon's Tepper School of Business are validating this fact. It's not just men who are needed to solve the world's problems and lead the world's nations. The world needs both genders—the entire image of God. Wooley writes, "The number of women on a given team influences that team's ability to solve complex problems."[8] We shouldn't be surprised that men and women in collaboration do better. It's God's true image after all.

God's trajectory has always been to make earth and heaven one. When that happens you can be sure as St. Paul once said that there will be "neither Jew nor Gentile, neither slave nor free, nor is there male and female, for you are all one in Christ Jesus" (Galatians 3:28).

One day we will sit together at the table of God. Not women on one side and men on the other. We will eat bread and drink wine undivided by gender, role, race or class. Take in what happens when we are all valued uniquely and just the same. It is the consummation of biblical history. On that day the beauty of God's image will shine like nothing we have ever seen. Until then it is our purpose and privilege to partner with God toward this end.

JOURNAL AND PRACTICE

1. What are the images that you have projected on God? What would it look like to let go of those projections and embrace the truth of Scripture? When we pray to God, most of us use images like Father, Shepherd, King, Lord. Are there other images of God that resonate with you? Create a list of other biblical images that expand your sense of God and use them when you pray.

2. As Renita Weems suggests, we are who we are because some mother, somewhere, stooped down long enough that we might climb on her back and ride piggyback into the future. Reflecting on your story, consider the women who have carried you. How have they been the face of God to you?

3. Where do you abdicate responsibility as an image bearer and culture maker? Where do you let a husband, father or male colleague do the work you have been charged to do? Take a step this week to own that place of responsibility given you as an image bearer. What are the obstacles in doing so? Talk to God and a soul friend or mentor about this.

4. Write a prayer of gratitude to God. Begin with the line, "Thank you God for making me a woman." What comes next? What flows from you as you open with that line? How hard or easy is it for you to write after that opening line?

5. If you are a woman who has a damaged and broken view of God as Father or Mother, look back at the images of God in this chapter. Does one image in particular resonate with you? Address a longing, a prayer or a part of your story to this image of God. What is that like for you?

6. Imagine God celebrating the divine image in you. What would God say to you? Make a list of the places God finds goodness and beauty in your life.

7. How does being a woman shape the story God is writing in your life? What are the particular gifts you bring with you into the journey? How do they reflect who God is?

GRATITUDES

❦

The very essence of this book is a group effort. Marshall McLuhan once said that "The medium is the message," and one message from this book has been the medium of togetherness on the project. Women collaborate. Friends and writing colleagues like Nancy Cremer, Karen Purcell, Dale Hanson Bourke and Lesa Engthaller contributed their six-word stories. Cindy Widmer, Julie Baier, Helen LaKelly Hunt, Marilyn Stewart, Linda Richardson, Nancy Cremer, Brandy Pardee, Amy McCurry, Heather Werle (a brilliant freelancer) and a few INKsters tweaked a chapter or two.

Adele was pulled away from her laptop by walking friends: Cynthia Snyder, Mary Henry, Kathryn Dietz, Janet Anthos, Rebecca Wasynczuk, Emily Nielsen Jones and Amy DiSanto. Other friends consistently shared the goodness of what happens when bread, wine and love are served: Barbara Shingleton, Tim and Michele Breene, Cynthia and Mark Snyder, Ross and Emily Jones. I (Adele) don't know how to write without friends who bring oxygen to my soul. Thank you, Deb Tall, Andrea Marshall, Pam Barker, Leslie Hillard, and Kim Dziama. Also, without Doug Calhoun's amazing cooking and encouragement as well as Annaliese, Nathaniel and Elie Calhoun's weekly check-ins I wouldn't have eaten or gone the distance. Huzzah for all of you.

I (Tracey) would be lost without the camaraderie and love of Amy McCurry, Nancy Cremer and Suanne Camfield, who care for my soul in ways beyond words. For Liz Reynolds, my sweet forever friend, and her constant encouragement about the project. Sassy Victoria Georgelos and Lisa Garvin and patient Jill Thackery-Proud, who always offer their help. For Constance, Rebecca and Sonia. And for caffeinated spin-class friends whose smiles and coffee time energize me so fully (Krista Waski and Lisa Chew). For my wise, patient and gracious husband, Joel (love you!), and my trio of adorable minions who had to wait to talk until "Mommy was off FaceTime with Miss Adele." And, of course, my own strong, stalwart mom and sister. Cindy Bunch showed grace when we were slow and prodded us toward the finish. We did it! And we had fun! And we are both grateful to the good people at Christ Church of Oak Brook and for the chance to share ministry together there. We were blessed by one another, with "face time." Thank you, God.

SMALL GROUP GUIDE

INTRODUCTION AND CHAPTER 1: YOUR ONE TRUE STORY—EXODUS 1:15-21

1. What messages have you heard about what you are "supposed" to be and do as a girl and then a woman?

2. When you reflect back on what movies (Disney or otherwise) shaped what you felt it meant to be a girl, what movies stand out to you?

3. What do you sense might be standing in the way of you becoming a more true you?

4. What was your experience with the journal and practice exercises like?

5. What Exodus experience(s) have you had?

6. The Pharaoh of Egypt was growing increasingly anxious as his Hebrew slaves began to grow in number and strength. Read Exodus 1:15-21. What do you sense life was like for a Hebrew woman under the new Pharaoh of Egypt?

7. What would it have been like to be a midwife at this time?

8. What sort of story would Shiphrah and Puah be telling about their lives?

9. Why, in Exodus 1:16, did Pharaoh let the girls live?

10. Why, in Exodus 1:17-19, did Shiphrah and Puah choose civil disobedience?

11. Where have you seen or experienced women coming together to stand against injustice, anger or greed like Shiphrah and Puah?

12. Where is God inviting you into a risky chapter of your story? What will you choose to do?

CHAPTER 2: TRUE SISTERS—RUTH 1:3-17

1. In Ruth 1:3-17, we take a peek into the lives of three women left on their own after the deaths of their husbands. What strikes you about Naomi's heart for her daughters-in-law?

2. Why does she work so hard to persuade them to make lives for themselves in Moab?

3. Have you ever had a friend you wanted to cling to until death? What was/is that like for you?

4. Why might God include this wonderful story of the friendship of two women in the Bible?

5. What has your experience with friendships been? What stories do you have of being used or cut as a friend, and what stories do you have of being invited into a sister's heart and journey? How do both inform the way you approach/befriend others today?

6. How do you let your friends know that you treasure their place in your life?

7. What is your experience around virtual connectivity? Facebook, Instagram, Twitter, Pinterest, Skype? What celebrations and/or tensions arise in your life from being connected through our virtual world?

8. What is it like for you to be face to face with a friend, to practice their presence and listen? What prevents you from engaging fully with people?

9. Are you intentionally investing yourself in the life of another sister? Why or why not? What has this been like for you?

10. What does it mean to you that Jesus calls you "friend"? How can you be a friend to Jesus?

CHAPTER 3: COMPETITORS OR COMRADES— PSALM 139:13-18

1. Psalm 139:13-18 provides a bedrock understanding of how God views us. What do you notice about God's perspective on you? Do you embrace this view or find it difficult to receive? Why?

2. Can you receive and appreciate the goodness of your created being the way God does? How might you begin to look at yourself through the eyes of God rather than the eyes of those around you?

3. How does an understanding of our objective, unchangeable value before God help us navigate comparison and competition?

4. How can we encourage other women to see themselves through the eyes of God and reinforce in them what God sees?

5. What happens inside you when you think of failing at something? Tease out these emotions and find which ones are of God and which harm and injure us.

6. How have you or those you loved experienced bullying? Consider bullying in light of Psalm 139. How does this passage challenge the behavior that brings about bullying?

7. What happens inside when you begin to compare yourself to others? How can you live in freedom from comparison so that you can live the full life God intends for you?

CHAPTER 4: CALL THE MIDWIFE!—LUKE 1:39-48

1. Both Mary and Elizabeth are surprised by their pregnancies. What reasons might Mary have had to visit Elizabeth?

2. How might have Elizabeth's reaction to seeing Mary grounded, encouraged and reassured her? How was she acting like a midwife to Mary's faith and growth?

3. When have you turned to another female friend in a time of stress? What was it like for you if that woman's perspective helped you navigate an intense time?

4. Mary responds to Elizabeth's encouragement with praise for what God is birthing in and through her. How might you respond with praise for what God is birthing in you?

5. Are you inviting others to share in your hardships and pain? Do you suffer in silence or bring others in? What do you tell yourself about the importance of doing or *not* doing this?

6. How has pain or hardship carved out new places in your soul? How have you found God, or how has God found you, in these times?

7. What do you make of Mother Teresa's words: "I have found the paradox, that if you love until it hurts, there can be no more hurt, only more love"?

CHAPTER 5: SHINY OBJECTS— 2 CORINTHIANS 10:13-18

1. In this passage we see that Paul was a driven achiever who worked tirelessly to establish churches among the Gentiles. Why does he emphasize his limits to the Corinthians? What is to be gained for the people by sharing his limits?

2. Paul knows which "field" is his and which is not. What is your field and what is not? Do you find yourself working in a field that is not yours to toil over?

3. Where do you stretch your limits, spin your abilities and what you have done, and try to look "larger than life"? What might Paul say to temptations to stretch ourselves wide?

4. How could being content with your limits and the Lord's commendation make you free?

5. How does the fear of missing out (FOMO) affect your life and the lives of people you love?

6. Do you have a hard time saying no to good things? How do you decide what you will and won't do?

7. How are you at practicing the present moment? How does the past, and what you should have said or done, or the future, with its to-do list, ambush you from being present to your limits?

8. What limits come with the life you have now? What would it mean to embrace them and find God in them?

9. What is one way you could begin today to be more present to your life and to those you love?

CHAPTER 6: INNER TRUTH—1 SAMUEL 25

1. In 1 Samuel 25:23-33 we read that "intelligent" and "beautiful" Abigail uses her voice to benefit many. What were the risks that Abigail took to confront David?

2. What do you learn about Abigail's character through the use of her voice?

3. How did Abigail's words affect her household and David's actions?

4. David blesses Abigail for her good judgment. Where is God inviting you to speak up with your good judgment? Is there a blessing there?

5. Where and when has your voice been either silenced or encouraged?

6. What does it mean to you that Jesus validated female voices in a society that intentionally diminished them?

7. What makes you most likely to abdicate your voice or hide your opinion? Is there any place you need to stand up and ask for what is fair, helpful or important in your life?

CHAPTER 7: HOW TO GIVE—AND RECEIVE—YOURSELF—JOHN 13:1-17

1. When Jesus gathers his disciples for the Last Supper he performs the task of a slave when he washes their filthy feet. Peter pushes back with Jesus. The intimacy is too much. How do you experience this passage and the intimacy Jesus is offering?

2. Jesus is asking Peter to lose his life in that moment so that he might gain something greater. That something greater takes Peter to a place of great leadership and strength in the church. What lessons are there for women in this story?

3. Women are often inclined to lay down their lives without asking what Jesus plans to do with us once we lay them down. Why do you think we often stay lying on the ground rather than dying to ourselves and then stepping up into what God has for us?

4. Why might it be easier to stay lying down rather than seek what God would have us step into?

5. Jesus' command to lose our lives so that we might find them is not a call to passivity; rather, it is a call to selfless action. It is an invitation to make ourselves humble and then find strength to act from that place. How do you see this humility and action working together in John 13?

6. Where are places that you sense God is asking you to submit your life? Where do you sense God is calling you to new action?

CHAPTER 8: 24/6 LIVING—EXODUS 20:1-17

1. The word *Sabbath* (*shabbat* in Hebrew) means "to cease" or "to rest." It is to stop striving and achieving and earning. Why is this such a foreign word to our Western lives today?

2. It is easy to dismiss the entire idea of Sabbath as archaic—an irrelevant heirloom in today's rapid-fire culture. How could a command given thousands of years ago to an obscure Semitic tribe address the pressures of technology, vocation and life today?

3. Do you currently have a Sabbath-keeping practice or have you ever tried to keep the Sabbath? What is/was your practice like for you?

4. God spends more time unpacking the Sabbath commandment than any of the other Ten Commandments. There are more words and details here than in any of the other nine. Why?

5. How do you sense that Sabbath keeping might look differently depending on your stage of life, socioeconomic status, urban or rural context, etc.? What makes Sabbath different for different people groups?

6. How does our willingness to keep this commandment honor God?

7. Nancy Beach once noted that the Sabbath is the only commandment that we brag about breaking. Why do we push God in this way? Why are we so proud if we keep at it?

8. How might your friends/family/community help you keep Sabbath? If you told them you wanted to keep this practice, what could they do to help you?

CHAPTER 9: APPROACHING GOD—GENESIS 32:22-30

1. Often we perpetuate myths about prayer. We believe that proper prayer comes with neatly folded hands, a quiet spirit, a silent place or eloquent words. What myths inform your view of prayer?

2. The Jewish patriarch Jacob struggled with God. It was an all-out wrestling match. Mary sang a "Magnificat" of praise. Prayer always happens in a context. What is your context? Right now, today, what is the situation in which you find yourself trying to pray?

3. Jacob wrestles with a "stranger" all night long. Eventually Jacob senses he is up against more than a man. He is wrestling with God. Have you ever felt as though you were wrestling with God over something? What was/is that like for you?

4. Why do we wrestle with God? What drives us to want something other than our current situation? What keeps us clinging, dragging our fists through the dirt of this life?

5. In this story, God gives Jacob a new name. The wrestling and striving lead to a new identity for God's people. Why was the renaming significant? What does a new name signify?

6. How do you sense God may be leading you to a different sort of prayer life? What might it look like for you to approach God differently than you have in the past?

7. Jacob had a reminder of his encounter with God; God touched his hip, and Jacob felt that reminder. What reminders do you carry with you of your encounters with God? Do they remind you of pain? joy? peace?

CHAPTER 10: TRUE WISDOM—ECCLESIASTES 3:1-15

1. As you consider the first eight verses, which season(s) do you sense that you may be in at the moment and which season(s) you have endured or enjoyed already? What lessons were learned in each?

2. Does the fact that "there is a time for everything" bring you a small glimmer hope or peace? Does it provide a resting stop for your mind and heart, or does it create anxiety or worry in you?

3. Ecclesiastes 3:11 tells us God has made everything beautiful in its time. What does that verse mean to you when you consider it in the context of youth, aging and the seasons of life?

4. Consider Ecclesiastes 3:15 in light of our culture, which lunges at

the next new idea or concept. What does this verse tell us about what is new and novel and where to expend our energies?

5. Life stages do not always happen in chronological order. We can provide wisdom and insight to women decades younger or older than us depending on what seasons we have moved though. Pick one "time" from this list that you have lived through and consider how you might use that season to encourage another woman.

6. Ecclesiastes 3:14 tells us that everything God does will endure forever. How does living with an eternal perspective help us move through the hard and late seasons of life?

CHAPTER 11: JUSTICE FOR ALL—GENESIS 21:8-20

1. When people talk about justice issues, what happens inside you? Do you resonate? feel apathetic or overwhelmed? experience compassion fatigue? intentionally pray?

2. Hagar is the third woman mentioned in the Bible by name. She lived at time when slavery was acceptable and common, yet God sees the unfairness of her life and makes her the same promise he gave Sarah and Abraham. In Genesis 21:8-20, what responses do Abraham and God give to the situation?

3. When God promises to make Ishmael into a great nation, what is communicated to Hagar and Ishmael about their status and worth?

4. Do you (or does someone you know) have a Hagar story to tell?

5. How might you be part of God's rescuing re-creation in the lives of women who are abused and unprotected? Does the Hagar/Ishmael story motivate you toward that end?

6. How could you stand in solidarity with a sister in need of resources, justice, protection or care?

7. What does helping God's kingdom come look like for you? God wants to see justice and hope in this world. What role are you to play in that end?

CHAPTER 12: TRUE IMAGE—GENESIS 1:26-31

1. What do you notice about the way God created both men and women in this passage?

2. In particular, what do you think it means when we read that God created both male and female and that all God made was "very good"?

3. When we read that women and men together reflect the image of God, does this encourage or overwhelm you?

4. If both men and women bear the image of God, does this change how you view or understand God?

5. Historically masculine images of God dominate the Christian landscape. What do men and women alike experience when we consider the other half of the image of God?

6. Scripture includes many passages that use female imagery to describe God. Does thinking of God as Mother connect with you? Why or why not?

7. What has your experience of bearing God's image been like? Have you felt respected and trusted as you bring your true you to conversations about God's image? Have you felt dismissed or "less than"? Consider telling a story about either experience.

RECOMMENDED RESOURCES

CHAPTER 1: YOUR ONE TRUE STORY
Books

Buster, Bobette. *Do Story: How to Tell Your Story So the World Listens.* A storyteller and screenwriter who consults with 20th Century Fox, Disney Animation, Sony Animation and Pixar Studios.

Dillard, Annie. *An American Childhood.* A master American storyteller and writer who helps us understand the beauty of story.

———. *The Maytrees.*

———. *Teaching a Stone to Talk.*

Green, John. *The Fault in Our Stars.* Adolescent fiction and bestselling book that reveals, by example, the art of storytelling in younger generations.

Lamott, Anne. *Traveling Mercies.* Anne Lamott tells her Exodus story with deprecating humor, vulnerability and love of God.

Linn, Matthew, Shiela Fabaricant Linn and Dennis Linn. *What Is My Song?* A beautiful storybook with pictures and an invitation to get in touch with your unique song.

Prior, Karen Swallow. *Booked: Literature in the Soul of Me.*

Winner, Lauren. *Girl Meets God.* An honest story of spiritual awakening and wondering by a brilliant woman and professor at Duke Divinity School.

Movies and Videos

The Tree of Life. Written and directed by Terrence Malick. The 2011 film moves between the origins and meaning of life and the memories of a middle-aged man's growing up in the 1950s.

Enchanted April. A wonderful movie set in the 1920s about four very different women making the journey to their true selves, to hope, to love and to friendship.

Websites

FullFill. www.fullfill.org. Faith-based digital magazine, webinars, weekly newsletter and other resources aimed at helping women "live out their influence."

The High Calling. www.thehighcalling.org. Daily devotional readings.

National Storytelling Festival. www.storytellingcenter.net/festival. Three days of listening to storytellers from all over the world spin out their tales.

The SALT Project. www.saltproject.org. A collection of poetry, art, photography and film to tell stories of our souls. Aimed at reclaiming the beauty of the Christian life through these mediums.

Six Words. www.sixwordmemoirs.com. A unique way to tell stories in just six words.

Story Chicago. http://storychicago.com/event. An annual conference that gathers storytellers from a variety of mediums together for a festival experience around telling your/our story and God's story.

CHAPTER 2: TRUE SISTERS

Books

Baab, Lynne M. *Friending: Real Relationships in a Virtual World.*

Bianchi, Tracey. *Mom Connection: Creating Vibrant Relationships in the Midst of Motherhood.* Tracey's second book on friendships during the harried season of motherhood.

Brestin, Dee. *The Friendships of Women.* A classic book on the topic from a well-known author and speaker.

Calhoun, Adele Ahlberg. *Invitations from God.* Look closely at the conversation in the introduction as well as chapter three, "An Invitation to Practice the Presence of People."

Caliguire, Mindy. *Spiritual Friendship.* Mindy has served as a ministry leader through the Willow Creek Association and leads a spiritual formation ministry called Soulcare.

Chittister, Joan. *Friendship of Women: The Hidden Tradition of the Bible.*

———. *The Story of Ruth: Twelve Moments in Every Woman's Life.*

Also consider these fiction reads on friendship. These titles often spark conversation for women in community or neighborhood book studies or small groups:

Horvath, Polly. *The Vacation.*

Kidd, Sue Monk. *The Secret Life of Bees.*

Stockett, Kathryn. *The Help*.

Movies and Videos

el-Wafi, Aicha, and Phyllis Rodriguez. TED Talk on Friendship. www
.ted.com/talks/9_11_healing_the_mothers_who_found_forgiveness_
friendship.html. The mother of conspirator Zacarias Moussaoui and
Phyllis Rodriguez, whose son was killed during the September 11 at-
tacks, discuss forgiveness.

Classic, feel good friendship movies also spark conversation on the topic:

Fried Green Tomatoes

Steel Magnolias

Toy Story

Bridesmaids

A League of Their Own

Divine Secrets of the Ya Ya Sisterhood

Websites

Rosalind Wiseman. Creating Cultures of Dignity. http://rosalind
wiseman.com.

Salamon, Maureen. "11 Interesting Effects of Oxytocin." www.livescience
.com/35219-11-effects-of-oxytocin.html. The effect of oxytocin on the
friendships of women.

CHAPTER 3: COMPETITORS OR COMRADES

Books

Sandberg, Sheryl. *Lean In: Women, Work and the Will to Lead*. A wonderful
read for women in the workforce by the COO of Facebook.

Wiseman, Rosalind. *Queen Bees and Wannabees: Helping Your Daughter
Survive Cliques, Gossip, Boyfriends, and the New Realities of Girl
World*.

————. *Master Minds and Wing Men: Helping Our Boys Cope with Schoolyard
Power, Locker-Room Tests, Girlfriends, and the New Rules of Boy World*.

Movies and Videos

Crow, Rachel. *Mean Girls*. www.youtube.com/watch?v=nTIBDuTxzUw.
Music video by Rachel Crow on bullying and loneliness as a girl.

Mean Girls. Tina Fey's cult classic.

Articles

"Mother of Bullied Teen Hopes to Change Florida's Laws." http:// usnews.nbcnews.com/_news/2014/01/17/22341028-mother-of-bullied -teen-hopes-to-change-floridas-laws?lite. A powerful story about a mom's attempts to put a stop to bullying.

CHAPTER 4: CALL THE MIDWIFE!

Books

Mains, Karen Burton. *Comforting One Another.* A wonderful book to give to those who are in pain.

Nouwen, Henri. *The Wounded Healer.*

Scazzero, Peter. *Emotionally Healthy Spirituality.* A great way to engage your soul in birthing something new.

Taylor, Barbara Brown. *When God Is Silent.* A good read for those who can't seem to hear God.

Young, William P. *The Shack.* A fiction story of pain, distrust, God's solidarity in bearing our load, and questions we leave for one another and for God.

Movies and Videos

Call the Midwife, PBS series. Based on the memoirs of Jennifer Worth, a midwife in the East End of London in the 1950s. If you haven't seen this we both recommend it. These episodes are filled with faith and presence and learning to hold pain and hope together.

Schwartzberg, Louie. TEDx talk. www.upworthy.com/clear-your-next -10-minutes-because-this-video-could-change-how-happy-you-are -with-your-entire-week. Louie Schwartzberg's visual perspective on the gifts of life using time-lapse photography. You can begin three minutes in if you simply want to watch the photography.

Websites

Pete Scazzero. www.petescazzero.com. Ministry resources aimed at helping people live emotionally healthy lives and raise up emotionally healthy churches.

CHAPTER 5: SHINY OBJECTS

Books

Caliguire, Mindy. *Simplicity.*

DeWaal, Esther. *Living with Contradictions.* This short book explores the paradoxes of living in the moment with presence.

Hart, Archibald, and Sylvia Frejd. *The Digital Invasion: How Technology Is Shaping You and Your Relationships.* Hart is a licensed psychologist and on faculty at Fuller Seminary. His work on anxiety and stress is telling.

Voskamp, Ann. *One Thousand Gifts.* This book has helped us become present to the lives we have. Adele has read it four times.

Movies and Videos

Limitless. Directed by Neil Burger. 2011. Great conversation starter about what a limitless life might actually look like.

Race to Nowhere: Leveraging the Power of Community to Transform Education. www.racetonowhere.com.

Articles

Hamilton, Jon. "Think You're Multi-tasking? Think Again." www.npr.org/templates/story/story.php?storyId=95256794. NPR Morning Edition piece on whether or not we can actually multitask.

March, Stephen. "Is Facebook Making Us Lonely?" *The Atlantic,* May 2012. Article about the pluses and perils of social media.

Naish, John. "Is Multi-tasking Bad for Your Brain?" www.dailymail.co.uk/health/article-1205669/Is-multi-tasking-bad-brain-Experts-reveal-hidden-perils-juggling-jobs.html.

Wortham, Jenna. "Feel Like a Wallflower? Maybe It's Your Facebook Wall." www.nytimes.com/2011/04/10/business/10ping.html?_r=0. *New York Times* article on social media and missing out.

CHAPTER 6: INNER TRUTH

Books

Beach, Nancy. *Gifted to Lead.* Nancy is a former teaching pastor and leader at Willow Creek Community Church who brings strong, insightful wisdom to conversations about women and leadership.

Belenky, Mary Field, Blythe Mcvicker Clinchy, Nancy Rule Goldberger and Jill Mattuck Tarule. *Women's Ways of Knowing: The Development of Self, Voice and Mind.* A secular classic.

Brown, Brene. *Daring Greatly: How the Courage to Be Vulnerable Transforms the Way We Live, Love, Parent and Lead.*

Cain, Susan. *Quiet: The Power of Introverts in a World That Can't Stop Talking.*

Carley, Linda L., and Alice H. Eagley. *Through the Labyrinth: The Truth About How Women Become Leaders.* An exploration of why women's paths to power remain difficult.

Lamott, Anne. *Bird by Bird.* This is the story of how a mom helps her son figure out how to get things done.

Uehlain, Brenda. *If You Want to Write.* This book is an oldie but goodie. Published in 1938, it provides an entertaining and instructive conversation on using your voice—even if you are not a writer.

Movies and Videos

Brown, Brene. "The Power of Vulnerability." TED Talk. www.ted.com/talks/brene_brown_on_vulnerability.html. This is a powerful talk on the beauty of vulnerability and how shame and fear keeps us from the things we most want

The Color Purple.

Erin Brockovich. Based on the true story of a woman who uses her voice and changes the face of a community.

Websites

Halee Gray Scott. www.hgscott.com/about. Scott's research on women in leadership is helpful and her book, *Dare Mighty Things* (2014), helps shape a great conversation on how women work and lead together.

Jenni Catron. www.jennicatron.com/about. Former executive director at Cross Point Church in Nashville, author and speaker.

CHAPTER 7: HOW TO GIVE—AND RECEIVE—YOURSELF

Books

Barton, Ruth Haley. *Longing for More: A Woman's Path to Transformation in Christ.* A lovely book on living into the truth of your purpose in life.

Johnson, Jan. *Abundant Simplicity: Discovering the Unhurried Rhythms of Grace.* An invitation to simplicity in speech, in what you own, in how you order your life and more.

McKnight, Scot. *The Blue Parakeet: Rethinking How You Read the Bible.* A great conversation on the way Jesus viewed and interacted with women.

Taylor, Barbara Brown. *The Seeds of Heaven: Sermons on the Gospel of Matthew.*

Movies and Videos

Bell, Rob. *She.* Nooma video.

Chan, Lisa. *True Beauty* films. A series of videos that create discussion around women's identity and the Bible.

Millions. A 2004 British comedy-drama directed by Danny Boyle. The story of two young boys and the different ways they handle a windfall of money. Their choices vividly express losing your life or hanging on to your life.

Websites

Adbusters. www.adbusters.org/campaigns/bnd. Canadian-based anti-consumerist, pro-environmental organization and magazine founded in 1989.

Buy Nothing Day. www.buynothingday.co.uk. An international day of protest against constant consuming.

Hagar's Sisters. www.hagarssisters.org. A Christian organization dedicated to resourcing those caught in the cycle of domestic abuse and those who know them.

The National Domestic Violence Hotline. www.thehotline.org. Immediate help and information on this struggle.

The Story of Stuff Project. www.storyofstuff.org. Almost three million people have watched this twenty-minute video about the underside of our compulsion to produce and consume around the clock.

CHAPTER 8: 24/6 LIVING

Books

Bass, Dorothy C. *Receiving the Day: Christian Practices for Opening the Gift of Time.* Offers an alternative to our attempts to manage and control time through attention, poetry, delight and presence.

Buchanan, Mark. *The Rest of God: Restoring Your Soul by Restoring Sabbath.*
A look at how the "rest of God" is an antidote to our crazy busy lives.

Dawn, Marva. *Keeping the Sabbath Wholly: Ceasing, Resting, Embracing, Feasting.* An exploration beyond sabbath as "going to church on Sunday."

———. *A Sense of the Call: A Sabbath Way of Life for Those Who Serve God, the Church and the World.* More on how sabbath touches every area of our lives.

Sleeth, Nancy. *Almost Amish: One Woman's Quest for a Slower, Simpler, More Sustainable Life.* A book on making conscious choices to limit oneself that can bring life.

Winner, Lauren. *Mudhouse Sabbath: An Invitation to a Life of Spiritual Discipline.* Winner converted from Judaism to Christianity. This book explores eleven Jewish practices that enrich our understanding and enjoyment of sabbath.

Movies and Videos

Interview with Pete Scazzero from New Life Church. http://newlifefellowship.org/learning/sabbath-resources. Pete knows the realities of how hard it is to stop, and he gives a reliable path into the practice of sabbath.

Websites

Center for A New American Dream. www.newdream.org. A fabulous organization aimed at helping people limit their consumption and spend time wisely.

CHAPTER 9: APPROACHING GOD

Books

Arthur, Sarah. *At the Still Point: A Literary Guide to Prayer in Ordinary Time.* A book on prayer that will appeal to the literature buff.

Calhoun, Adele Ahlberg. *Spiritual Disciplines Handbook.* Explore the many paths to prayer found here, including healing prayer, contemplative prayer, breath prayer, conversational prayer, intercession and centering prayer.

Lamott, Anne. *Help, Thanks, Wow.* A sometimes irreverent book about how Anne has learned to connect with God in a simple yet profound way.

Linn, Dennis, Matthew Linn and Shiela Fabricant Linn. *Making Heart-Bread*. A wonderful picture book of how to be present to God.

Loder, Ted. *Guerrillas of Grace*. These fantastic prayers are perfect for crisis or everyday numbness toward God.

Macbeth, Sybil. *Praying in Color: Drawing a New Way to God*. A resource for the visual or kinesthetic learner who runs out of words to pray.

Taylor, Barbara Brown. *An Altar in this World*. A journey into how our natural everyday life is riddled with God and the sacred.

Movies and Videos

The Apostle. A film written and directed by Robert Duvall, 1997. The story gets at how God uses broken people for the sake of the kingdom.

Tender Mercies. Directed by Bruce Beresford, 1983. A recovering alcoholic converts to Christianity.

Websites

Mindy Caliguire's Soul Care Resources. www.soulcare.com. Videos, articles and resources on the spiritual journey.

Praying in Color. www.prayingincolor.com. A host of resources that use the imagination and even a doodle to pray.

The writings and resources of Phyllis Tickle. www.phyllistickle.com/books. Resources for prayer and a host of related issues.

Apps

The Divine Hours. "Explore Faith" app. A free app for your phone that provides a way of praying the Divine Hours.

CHAPTER 10: TRUE WISDOM

Books

Ephron, Nora. *I Feel Bad About My Neck and Other Thoughts on Being a Woman*. A book to make you laugh at the realities of aging.

Hagberg, Janet O., and Robert A. Guelich. *The Critical Journey*. A study on the major learning and challenges for each stage of life.

Sawyer, Joy. *Dancing to the Heartbeat of Redemption*. Sawyer uses poetry to get at the spiritual journey.

Viorst, Judith. *Necessary Losses: The Loves, Illusions, Dependencies and Impossible Expectations That All of Us Have to Let Go of to Grow*. The title says it all. A researched study of how learning to grieve losses is part of the fabric of our lives.

Movies and Videos

Ed's Story. www.edsstory.com. A short film series featuring Ed Dobson and his journey with ALS.

Mom's Night Out. A 2014 comedy about moms and the harried stage of life.

CHAPTER 11: JUSTICE FOR ALL

Books

Bancroft, Lundy. *Why Does He Do That? Inside the Minds of Angry Men*. This book was part of a course I took to understand domestic abuse. It was eye opening and helpful.

Kristof, Nicholas, and Sheryl WuDunn. *Half the Sky: Turning Oppression into Opportunity for Women Worldwide*. A riveting book on one of the most important global issues of our time.

Milway, Katie Smith. *The Good Garden: How One Family Went from Hunger to Having Enough*. Milway's wonderful children's books teach children how to engage with a world in need.

———. *Mimi's Village: And How Basic Health Care Transformed It*.

———. *One Hen: How One Small Loan Made a Big Difference*.

Taylor, Barbara Brown. *Speaking of Sin: The Lost Language of Salvation*. A series of sermons on the brokenness of this world and the hope that is found in Jesus.

Movies and Videos

Girl Rising. www.girlrising.com/see-the-film/about-the-film. A film tracing the challenges and desires that girls face in various parts of our world. The hunger for education and voice is riveting.

Half the Sky Movement. www.halftheskymovement.org. PBS Documentary that brings to life the stories of girls in the book *Half the Sky*.

Lyn Lusi's Opus Prize Acceptance Speech for her work with Heal Africa. http://vimeo.com/36715843.

Charles Malik address. http://espace.wheaton.edu/bgc/video/cn003V1and2 -malik.html. In 1980, the Billy Graham Center at Wheaton College was dedicated. The speaker was Dr. Charles Malik from Lebanon, whose words became legend for scolding evangelicals for their anemic social action.

"The Girl Who Silenced the World for 6 Minutes," www.youtube.com/watch?v=d7ep_8SLQho. Severn Suzuki, founder of Ecological Children's Organization (ECO), speaks at the 1992 UN Earth Summit. A girl's plea to take care of our planet's health for the sake of the generations to come.

Websites

Evangelical Environmental Network. www.creationcare.org. Offering resources for creation care.

The International Justice Mission. www.ijm.org. IJM has been involved in changing legislation that represses women and turns a blind eye toward trafficking.

Moms Rising. www.momsrising.org.

One Hen. www.onehen.org. This is a fun interactive website showing children what they can do about global issues.

She Loves Magazine. www.shelovesmagazine.com/2014/stop-silence-start-healing-initiative. Amy Rasmussen Buckley addresses issues of violence toward women.

Sojourners. www.sojo.net/magazine. A magazine about issues of social justice.

Whitby Forum. www.whitbyforum.com. Addresses issues of women in the church and wider world.

World Vision. www.worldvision.org.

CHAPTER 12: TRUE IMAGE

Books

Blue, Debbie. *Consider the Birds.*

James, Carolyn Custis. *Half the Church: Recapturing God's Global Vision for Women.* Addresses who women are in Christ and offers hope for changing the plight of women worldwide.

Johnson, Alan F. *How I Changed My Mind About Women in Leadership: Compelling Stories from Prominent Evangelicals.* A compendium of

stories by Christians who changed their minds on what women can
and cannot do. Voices include John and Nancy Ortberg, Tony
Campolo, Lynne Hybels and others.

Liefield, Walter, and Ruth A. Tucker. *Daughters of the Church*. A fascinating account of women's stories in the church, spanning two
thousand years.

Sayers, Dorothy. *Are Women Human?* A sensible approach to the discussion about men's and women's roles that looks at their similarities,
not just their differences.

Articles

Burkus, David. "Need Better Ideas? Ask More Women." www.psycholo
gytoday.com/blog/creative-leadership/201404/need-better-ideas-ask
-more-women. This article highlights what women bring to the mix.

Interview with Pope Francis, by Antonio Spadaro, S.J. September 30, 2013.
www.americamagazine.org/pope-interview. In this interview the pope
voices the need for women's voices in the decision-making process: "The
feminine genius is needed wherever we make important decisions."

Websites

Christianity Today's Her.meneutics. www.christianitytoday.com/women.
Christianity Today blogs and posts for women.

Christians for Biblical Equality. www.cbeinternational.org. CBE advances gift-based rather than gender-based service within the church
and the world.

The Junia Project. www.juniaproject.com and www.facebook.com/junia
project. This alliance works to support gender equality in the church
and offers virtual community and practical resources.

The Synergy Women's Network. www.facebook.com/SynergyWomens
Network.

Ann Vyn's Theology Connect blog post on patriarchy: http://theology
connect.wordpress.com/2014/01/25/the-patriarchal-shame-connect.

FOR THE MEN

While we were writing this book, a guy in Adele's congregation asked if he could read it. Adele suggested he go for it, but followed up with, "I'm not sure you will like it."

His response, "I have enjoyed all your other books, and I want to understand women. So why wouldn't I read it!?"

We are so grateful for men with hearts that are open to hearing what women have to say. If you are one of those men, thank you on behalf of women finding their way toward their truest selves.

Tracey works at a church that empowers women to lead and serve in marvelous ways. Both inside churches and in the marketplace, in boardrooms, the healthcare industry, colleges, etc., where men view women as equal partners and comrades, we are grateful.

If you are a guy, here are a few ways you might engage with this book:

1. If you are in a book club, classroom or small group setting with women, read a chapter a week and discuss it together. How do men view the ideas and concepts presented in similar or different ways than the women?

   - What do you learn about women that you haven't noticed before?

   - What principles and practices speak to both men and women, principles that ring true for both genders?

   - What do you learn about yourself?

   - What sort of call does each chapter place on your life? Do certain ideas and concepts nudge you to consider acting, thinking or working differently?

2. If you are married, consider reading this book with your wife. Invite her to tell you her reactions to each chapter. What do you learn about her? Share your own responses.

- Are there ways that what you are reading can shape your marriage?

- Do you have a daughter or niece who might benefit from your reading of this book? How do you see her struggling or succeeding as she seeks to bring her true self to the table?

3. If you are reading this book on your own, take on some of the practices. Many are timeless practices culled from both men and women who have gone the road before us. The practices can also work for you.

4. Consider your own personal contexts or communities. Where are women in need of hope, encouragement or an opportunity to use their voices? Can you help crack open a space for them? Men and women alike have the responsibility to help bring out the true selves and stories of our lives and others' lives. Can you help make that happen? Where do women need advocates, mentors, and men with love and power to align with God's vision for a new creation? What might you do?

5. If you are a pastor, consider the fact that in most churches, 50 to 60 percent of your congregation is female. What does your church do well that helps encourage them? What might your church do better to help women find their true selves in Christ?

NOTES

INTRODUCTION

[1]Suzanne Heintz, "Life Once Removed," accessed July 15, 2014, at www.suzan neheintz.com/life-once-removed.

[2]"Women and Depression," National Alliance on Mental Illness, accessed July 15, 2014, at www.nami.org/Content/NavigationMenu/Mental_Illnesses /Depression/Women_and_Depression/Women_and_Depression_Facts.htm.

[3]John Donne, *Devotions upon Emergent Occasions*, http://web.cs.dal.ca/~johnston /poetry/island.html.

[4]Suzanne Heintz, "Life Once Removed."

CHAPTER 1: YOUR ONE TRUE STORY

[1]Bechdel Test Movie List, accessed April 28, 2014, at www.bechdeltest.com.

[2]Shelby Knox, "Introducing the Radical Women's History Project," accessed July 15, 2014, at http://shelbyknox.wordpress.com/2011/01/04/introducing -the-radical-womens-history-project.

[3]Helen LaKelly Hunt, *The Half-Moon Book: Reflections on the Power Within*, unpublished PhD thesis, p. 33.

[4]Douglas Brinkley, "Rosa Parks," accessed on April 28, 2014, at www.nytimes .com/books/first/b/brinkley-parks.html.

CHAPTER 2: TRUE SISTERS

[1]Emily Dickinson, *Poems by Emily Dickenson, Three Series, Complete*, ed. Mabel Loomis Todd and T. W. Higginson. Open source Kindle Edition, F 71 (1859) 92.

[2]Claire Luchette, "6 of the Best Friendship Quotes from Funny Women," accessed April 28, 2014, at www.bustle.com/articles/7639-6-of-the-best -friendship-quotes-from-funny-women.

[3]Anne Lamott, *Traveling Mercies: Some Thoughts On Faith* (New York: Random House, 1999); accessed April 28, 2014, at www.goodreads.com /work/quotes/14837-traveling-mercies-some-thoughts-on-faith.

[4]James Strong, *Strong's Exhaustive Concordance of the Bible* (Nashville: Thomas Nelson, 2009), s.v. 6440.

[5]*Les Misérables*; from "Quotes for Jean Valjean," accessed April 28, 2014, at www.imdb.com/character/ch0014450/quotes.

[6]Gale Berkowitz, "UCLA Study on Friendship Among Women," accessed on April 28, 2014, at www.anapsid.org/cnd/gender/tendfend.html.

[7]Maureen Salamon, "11 Interesting Effects of Oxytocin," accessed on April 28, 2014, at www.livescience.com/35219-11-effects-of-oxytocin.html.

CHAPTER 3: COMPETITORS OR COMRADES

[1]Sheryl Sandburg, *Lean In: Women, Work and the Will to Lead* (New York: Alfred A. Knopf, 2013), p. 24.

[2]Stephen Gandel, "Are Women Less Competitive Than Men? Explaining the Gender Gap," *Time*, November 30, 2010, http://business.time .com/2010/11/30/are-women-less-competitive-than-men-explaining-the -gender-gap.

[3]Ibid.

[4]Lee Dye, "Men Crave Competition, in Work and Play," ABC News, January 19, 2011, http://abcnews.go.com/Technology/DyeHard/men-crave-compe tition-women-work-play/story?id=12641830.

[5]Katherine Crowley and Kathi Elster, "Men vs. Women: Why the Work Divide Matters," *Upstart Business Journal*, January 10, 2013, http://upstart .bizjournals.com/resources/author/2013/01/10/male-versus-female-behavior -at-work.html?page=all.

[6]C. Joybell C., "C. Joybell C. Quotes," accessed on April 28, 2014, at www .goodreads.com/author/quotes/4114218.C_JoyBell_C_?page=10Goodreads.

CHAPTER 4: CALL THE MIDWIFE!

[1]Emilie Griffin, *Souls in Full Sail: A Christian Spirituality for the Later Years* (Downers Grove, IL: InterVarsity Press, 2011), p. 120.

[2]*Enhanced Strong's Lexicon* (Oak Harbor, WA: Logos Research Systems, 1995).

[3]Gerhard Kittel, Gerhard Friedrich and Geoffrey William Bromiley, ed., *Theological Dictionary of the New Testament, Volume 1* (Grand Rapids: William B. Eerdmans Publishing Company, 1985), p. 1258.

[4]Brene Brown, "The Power of Vulnerability," TED Talk, June 2010, www.ted .com/talks/brene_brown_on_vulnerability.

CHAPTER 5: SHINY OBJECTS

[1]Stephen Marche, "Is Facebook Making Us Lonely?" *The Atlantic*, May 2012, www.theatlantic.com/magazine/archive/2012/05/is-facebook-making-us -lonely/308930.

[2]John Nash, "Is Multi-Tasking Bad for Your Brain? Experts Reveal the Hidden

Perils of Juggling Too Many Jobs," MailOnline.com, August 11, 2009, www.dailymail.co.uk/health/article-1205669/Is-multi-tasking-bad-brain -Experts-reveal-hidden-perils-juggling-jobs.html.

CHAPTER 7: HOW TO GIVE—AND RECEIVE—YOURSELF

[1]For more information, visit www.buynothingday.co.uk.

[2]Chuck Colson, "Domestic Violence Within the Church: The Ugly Truth," *BreakPoint,* October 20, 2009, www.christianheadlines.com/news/domestic -violence-within-the-church-the-ugly-truth-11602500.html.

[3]Barbara Brown Taylor, *Seeds of Heaven* (Louisville: Westminster John Knox Press, 2004), p. 80.

[4]Ibid., p. 79.

CHAPTER 8: 24/6 LIVING

[1]Juliet B. Schor, *The Overworked American* (New York: BasicBooks, 1992), p. 5.

[2]Matthew Sleeth, "Living 24/6 in a 24/7 World," OnFaith, October 31, 2012, www.faithstreet.com/onfaith/2012/10/31/living-246-in-a-247-world/11159. See also his book *24/6: Prescription for a Healthier, Happier Life* (Carol Stream, IL: Tyndale House, 2012).

CHAPTER 9: APPROACHING GOD

[1]Anne Lamott, *Help, Thanks, Wow: The Three Essential Prayers* (New York: Penguin, 2012); accessed on April 28, 2014, at www.goodreads.com/work /quotes/21421044-help-thanks-wow-three-essential-prayers.

[2]Sybil MacBeth, *Praying in Color: Drawing a New Path to God* (Brewster, MA: Paraclete Press, 2007).

[3]Barbara Brown Taylor, *An Altar in the World: A Geography of Faith* (New York: HarperCollins, 2009), p. 176.

[4]Adele Calhoun, *The Spiritual Disciplines Handbook* (Downers Grove, IL: InterVarsity Press, 2005).

[5]Anne Lamott, *Help, Thanks, Wow.*

[6]The Book of Common Prayer.

[7]Emilie Griffin, *Souls in Full Sail* (Downers Grove, IL: InterVarsity Press, 2010), p. 83.

[8]Dan Graves, "Article #31," accessed on April 29, 2014, at www.christian historyinstitute.org/incontext/article/julian.

CHAPTER 10: TRUE WISDOM

[1]"Life in my 40s: 'I Need to Take My Pants Off as Soon as I Get Home,'" www.courierpress.com/lifestyle/life-in-my.

[2]Nora Ephron, *I Feel Bad About My Neck: and Other Thoughts on Being a Woman* (New York: Alfred A. Knopf, 2006), pp. 3, 7.

CHAPTER 11: JUSTICE FOR ALL

[1]Human Trafficking Statistics: Polaris Project, accessed on April 28, 2014, at www.cicatelli.org/titlex/downloadable/Human%20Trafficking%20 Statistics.pdf.

[2]"11 Facts About Global Poverty," accessed on April 29, 2014, at www .dosomething.org/facts/11-facts-about-global-poverty.

[3]Associated Press, "Number of U.S. children living in poverty increases to a staggering 23 per cent in wake of recession, survey reveals," accessed April 29, 2014, at www.dailymail.co.uk/news/article-2347649/Number-U-S -children-living-poverty-increases-23-percent-wake-recession-Survey.html.

[4]"30,000 Children Die Each Day from Preventable Diseases," accessed April 28, 2014, at www.realnews24.com/30000-children-die-each-day -from-preventable-diseases.

[5]ABC News Staff, "100 Million Dieters, $20 Billion: Weight-Loss Industry by the Numbers," accessed April 28, 2014, at http://abcnews.go.com/Health /100-million-dieters-20-billion-weight-loss-industry/story?id=16297197.

[6]Brene Brown, "Daring Greatly," accessed on April 28, 2014, at www.womenin focus.com.au/docs/DOC-2850.

[7]Nicholas D. Kristof and Sheryl WuDunn, *Half the Sky* (New York: Vintage Books, 2010), p. xiii.

[8]Barbara Taylor Brown, *Speaking of Sin: The Lost Language of Salvation* (Cambridge, MA: Cowley Publications, 2000), p. 77.

CHAPTER 12: TRUE IMAGE

[1]"Antimicrobial Resistance," World Health Organization, April 2014, http:// who.int/mediacentre/factsheets/fs194/en.

[2]Ian Muir-Cochrane, "Are there really 21 million slaves worldwide?," accessed April 29, 2014, at www.bbc.com/news/magazine-26513804.

[3]*Mishneh Torah*, Tefilah and Birkat Kohanim, Chapter Seven, trans. Eliyahu Touger (Moznaim Publications), www.chabad.org/library/article_cdo /aid/920169/jewish/Tefilah-and-birkat-kohanim-chapter-seven.htm.

[4]Dorothy Sayers, *Are Women Human? Penetrating, Sensible, and Witty Essays on the Role of Women in Society* (Grand Rapids: Eerdmans, 1971).

[5]Myra and David Sadker, "The Impact of Sexism in Schools," *Wisconsin Academy Review* 19, no. 2 (1973): 4.

[6]Catechism of the Catholic Church, Concacan Inc. Libreria Editrice Vaticana, Citta del Vaticano, 1992. Published by the Canadian Conference of Catholic Bishops, Ottawa, Ontario, p. 60.

[7]Reneta Weems, *Just a Sister Away: Understanding the Timeless Connection Between Women of Today and Women in the Bible* (New York: Warner Books, 2007).

[8]David Burkus, "Need Better Ideas? Ask More Women," *Psychology Today*, April 7, 2014, www.psychologytoday.com/blog/creative-leadership/201404 /need-better-ideas-ask-more-women.

Other good reads by Adele Ahlberg Calhoun

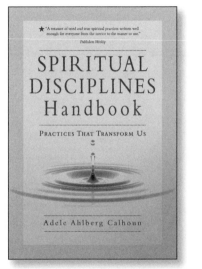

IVP *Crescendo*
COURAGE. CONFIDENCE. CALLING.

Some voices challenge us. Others support or encourage us. Voices can move us to change our minds, draw close to God, discover a new spiritual gift. The voices of others are shaping who we are.

The voices behind IVP Crescendo join together to draw us into God's story. We'll discover God's work around the globe even as we learn to love the people around the corner. We'll have opportunity to heal our places of pain. We'll discover new ways to love our families. We'll hear God's voice speaking into our lives as we discover new places of influence.

IVP Crescendo invites you to join in the rising chorus

- *to listen to the voices of others*
- *to hear the voice of God*
- *and to grow your own voice in*

COURAGE. CONFIDENCE. CALLING.

ivpress.com/crescendo
ivpress.com/crescendo-social